Living Baptism Daily

Lawrence E. Mick

LITURGICAL PRESS
Collegeville, Minnesota

www.litpress.org

	2	3	4	5	6	7	8

Library of Congress Cataloging-in-Publication Data

Mick, Lawrence E., 1946–
    Living baptism daily / Lawrence E. Mick.
        p.   cm.
    Includes bibliographical references.
    ISBN 0-8146-2965-2 (pbk. : alk. paper)
    1. Baptism.   I. Title.

BV811.3.M53   2004
234'.161—dc22   2003026730

Contents

Preface

One of the more interesting and largely unanticipated side effects of the reintroduction of the catechumenate into the life of the Catholic Church has been the number of active members of the parish who have come forward saying that they need something like the catechumenate process for their own spiritual lives. Those who enter the church through the Rite of Christian Initiation of Adults commonly manifest such enthusiasm for and understanding of their faith that "cradle Catholics" sense that they have missed something.

This book is intended to help meet that felt need for the already baptized. It does not seek to create some kind of parish structure parallel to the catechumenate, but it seeks to help those who are already members of the Order of the Faithful to tap into the power of the catechumenate experience. Examining the dynamics and stages and rituals of the Rite of Christian Initiation of Adults provides the basis for a deepened understanding of the meaning of baptism. The way any group initiates its new members expresses how that group understands itself and its purpose. It spells out in a variety of ways the meaning of membership in the group and what is expected of every member.

For those already baptized, therefore, reflecting on how the Church initiates adults and children of catechetical age offers renewed and expanded awareness of the meaning of

Christian initiation and thus of church membership. A more frequent awareness of the fact that one is baptized and of the implications that being baptized has for daily living can be a significant factor leading to a fuller and richer living of the Christian life.

Through baptism, confirmation, and Eucharist, we are initiated into the mystery of life in Christ. This mystery can never be fully comprehended nor can its richness be exhausted. We are called by God, however, to grow ever more fully into this life in Christ and thus to experience the mystery more deeply as we grow in faith. My hope is that this work will help many members of the Church in that process.

Each chapter of the book includes material for prayer drawn from the *Rite of Christian Initiation of Adults* or from the *Sacramentary*. Some of these texts are clearly prayers for the catechumens or the elect and may be prayer for them; they could also easily be adapted by changing a few words to become prayers for those already baptized. Questions for personal reflection and/or for group discussion also follow each chapter. Finally, suggestions for use of the material by parish leadership, linked to each chapter, may be found in the appendix. This material should enable parish leaders to apply the reflections to their own lives in the Church and to imagine a variety of ways of enhancing parishioners' awareness of their baptismal status and its implications for daily living.

1

Fresh from the Font

One Easter Sunday after church services, the minister stood at the door shaking hands as the congregation departed.

As one man shook his hand, the minister pulled him aside. "You need to join the Army of the Lord," the minister said emphatically.

The man looked surprised. "I'm already in the Army of the Lord, Pastor," he said.

"How come I don't see you except for Christmas and Easter?" asked the minister.

The man leaned toward the minister's ear and whispered, "I'm in the secret service."

Too many baptized Christians seem to belong to such a secret service. Though claiming membership in the Church, they show little evidence that their baptism has made much difference in the way they live. We baptize adults, after months or even years of preparation, and discover that some disappear from the parish after their baptism. Often we baptize infants whose parents neglect to bring them to church after they have been baptized, so that they are not really raised as active members of the Church.

This is not the way baptism is supposed to work. Yet far too often, baptism does not seem to achieve its goals. For too many Christians it is a past event that has minimal impact on the way they live their daily lives. Even among fervent members of the Church, there is often little conscious connection between the sacrament through which their lives in Christ began and the living of the Christian life after baptism.

At the Bottom of It All

It seems to me that this lack of vital baptismal consciousness lies at the root of many, perhaps most, of the problems that we face in parish life. I first began working with the Rite of Christian Initiation of Adults in 1974, and I have devoted much time and energy in the years since that time to its implementation in parish life. My motivation for taking the catechumenate so seriously is that I think it holds the key to revitalizing the Church's awareness of the meaning of baptism and thus the meaning of Christian identity and the shape of Christian life.

Not long after my ordination as a priest in 1972, I began realizing how the challenges we faced in renewing parishes were frequently linked to this lack of baptismal awareness.

Why, for example, do only a minority of parishioners regularly support the Church financially? Why do so few use their envelopes, and why do many who do use them give so little? It seems to me that this pattern indicates a lack of ownership of the Church's mission and a corresponding lack of responsibility for making the work of the Church possible financially.

Even where parishioners support the local parish generously, why do so many of them decline to support the overseas missions or the home mission societies? Does it not flow from a lack of commitment to the work of evangelization that Christ entrusted to the Church, a mission given to each of the baptized?

Beyond finances, it is a common assumption in parish life that a small minority, perhaps 20 percent, of parishioners do all the work in the parish. Why are the majority not willing to give their time and effort to carrying on the work of the parish? Why do they assume that such involvement is simply an issue of personal choice, an optional matter for those inclined to volunteer? Does this not reveal a lack of recognition that baptism calls all of us to responsibility for the life and the mission of the Church?

Some of this, of course, flows from the assumption that the work of the Church is really the responsibility of the clergy. Thus when people do volunteer, they see it as "helping the pastor" and expect to be thanked for their assistance. Does this not indicate a devaluing of the significance of baptism with the concurrent assumption that the clergy are really the Church?

A similar assumption affects the liturgical life of the parish. Too many parishioners assume that the worship of the Church is the responsibility of the clergy. Participation is also seen as a matter of personal choice. If people like to sing, they can sing. If not, they can remain silent. Participation is another form of volunteer activity—and the pastor should be grateful to those who choose to participate. Does not this attitude reflect a lack of understanding that baptism is the basis for our participation in worship and that the whole Church bears responsibility for giving proper praise to God?

The same pattern reveals itself when parents assume that the religious education of their children is the responsibility of the parish school or the parish religion program. The assumption is that catechesis is the responsibility of the professional religious (or at least the active volunteers). Does this not indicate a lack of awareness that baptism includes responsibility for handing on the faith to the next generation?

The lack of family-based formation in the faith also leads to an inadequate development of conscience. Too many Christians today form their moral sensibility on the basis of societal standards rather than on solid moral theology. Why do surveys so often show that Christians hold the same position on many moral issues as the society at large? Does this not indicate a lack of awareness that baptism sets us apart and calls us to a life based on gospel values rather than the values of the world?

The values of the world also seem to shape many Christians' approach to marriage. Why do so many marriages fail today? Why do so many couples being married want a wedding that is more style show than worship? Is it not, at least in part, a result of not understanding marriage as a vocation, as a way of living out one's baptismal commitment in the Church?

A similar issue may underlie the developing shortage of ordained ministers in the Church. Ordination is another way of living out one's baptismal vocation. If that baptismal commitment is weak, then responding to God's call to serve the Church in holy orders is less likely.

Celebrating in Public

Our general lack of baptismal awareness flows, at least in great part, from our past baptismal practice. The fact that most of us were baptized as infants means that we have no personal memories of our own baptisms. This need not be a major obstacle, however, if parents make it a point to celebrate the anniversaries of their children's baptisms as they grow up. Using the baptismal candle, viewing photos or videos of the event, and having a party would help a child develop a strong awareness of the significance of his or her baptism.

More detrimental to awareness than our practice of infant baptism has been the custom of celebrating baptism in relative isolation. Infant baptisms were commonly (and in many places still are) celebrated on Sunday afternoon with only the godparents and immediate family present. Adult baptisms were performed almost in secret, lest those being baptized be embarrassed for not having been baptized as infants. In both cases, the parish as a whole was excluded. Many church members grew up without ever seeing a baptism unless they were involved in the baptism of a close relative. Baptism fell victim to the old adage: "Out of sight, out of mind."

The renewal of the initiation sacraments after the Second Vatican Council has begun to bring baptism out of the shadows. Infant baptisms are often (at least in some parishes) celebrated during Sunday Mass so that the whole assembly can share in the celebration of new life in the community. Fostering that practice is one very effective way to increase baptismal awareness in a parish.

Even more powerful in fostering this awareness, however, is the full implementation of the Rite of Christian Initiation of Adults. Parishes who have taken seriously the proper use of this rite (issued from Rome in 1972) have discovered its profound impact on the vitality of the parish and the self-identity of its members.

Part of the reason that the experience of adult initiation has such a strong effect is that it involves adults and children of catechetical age, so members of the assembly can relate the experience of the initiates to their own lives more directly than they can with infant baptism.

Another reason for the effectiveness of the RCIA is the length of the process of formation that the rite requires. While the baptism of an infant may capture the attention of the assembly for the length of a Sunday Mass, the initiation of catechumens requires their involvement with the community over a period longer than a year. (The U.S. Statutes for the RCIA require at least a full year for the periods of the catechumenate proper and purification and enlightenment. Added to these are the periods of inquiry and mystagogy, which respectively precede and follow the central two periods.)

Moreover, this process is designed to be shared with the whole community in a series of ritual moments that mark the progress of the catechumens (along with candidates for full communion who may accompany them). Beyond the ritual moments, the catechumens and candidates are supposed to be involved with the life of the community in a variety of ways: in various prayer experiences, in service to others both inside and outside the church membership, and in social events that enable the initiates to get to know and be known by other members of the parish.

All of this community interaction enables the members of the assembly to support and guide the initiates as they learn the Christian way of life. It also allows the community to share in the initiation journey of the catechumens, and thus it invites those already baptized to renew their own conversion. This communal renewal is ritually expressed at Easter with the renewal of baptismal vows by the whole assembly in union with those baptized at the Easter Vigil.

Not all parishes, of course, have fully implemented the Rite of Christian Initiation of Adults. Too often it remains on the sidelines, offering much care and instruction for the initiates but not involving many of the members of the assembly in the process. Even minimal implementation has some effect, for the process is still more public than the pre-conciliar pattern of baptism in secret. Full implementation of the vision of the RCIA, however, brings it to the center of parish life. When this happens, the effects on the whole assembly are both profound and exciting.

Unlocking the Power

The potential impact of the RCIA on parish life was recognized very early by Fr. Aidan Kavanagh, O.S.B. In an article in *Worship* in 1974, he predicted its historic effects:

> From the admittedly poor vantage point of the present, however, I would hazard that this document may well appear to a writer a century from now as the most important result of the Second Vatican Council for the life

of the church. I hazard this, not because of the document's ceremonial details but because of the concrete, robust, and disciplined vision it projects of the church as a community of faith lived in common—a vision it means to be efficaciously enacted over and over again, each year at the center of the church's being as it corporately passes, in Jesus Christ, from death to life by the Spirit.[1]

Full implementation of the rite creating a vital catechumenate is, of course, the main key to unlocking the power of the RCIA. Ritual creates its effects by being celebrated well. There is no substitute that will compensate for poor celebration.

When the rites are celebrated well, however, there is also value to reflecting on the celebrations to unpack their deeper meanings and to discern their implications for ongoing life in Christ. That is the purpose of post-baptismal or mystagogical catechesis—to unpack the meaning of "the mysteries," which is an ancient term for sacraments. The RCIA focuses mystagogy during the Fifty Days of Easter, but the U.S. statutes also call for an extended mystagogy lasting at least a year.

In a broader sense, however, mystagogy is really a life-long process. No matter at what age we were initiated into the Christian life, we will spend the rest of our lives figuring out what happened to us and what it all meant. Ultimately all catechesis after initiation is mystagogical catechesis.

The chapters in this book are intended as an aid to such catechesis. They are designed to help Christians probe more deeply into their identity as members of the people of God. What does it mean to be counted among the baptized? What are the implications of baptism for daily life? What distinguishes the baptized from the unbaptized? How are we to live once we have been baptized? What demands does baptism place

---

[1] Aidan Kavanagh, "Christian Initiation of Adults: The Rites," *Worship* (June–July, 1974) 335.

upon us? What rights and privileges does baptism convey? How are we to live once we have been baptized? These are the kinds of questions this book will seek to probe.

Aidan Kavanagh has called the adult catechumenate the "norm" for Christian initiation. This does not mean that most new members of the Church will be initiated as adults. It implies, rather, that our understanding of the meaning of baptism is to be based on the adult experience of conversion and celebration. Infant baptism, while clearly legitimate, is also clearly an adaptation of the adult experience. To properly understand the significance of baptism, we begin with the catechumenate.

The process and the rituals that are outlined in the Rite of Christian Initiation of Adults, then, will provide the basis for our reflections. In the course of this work, we will reflect on the basic dynamics of the catechumenate experience and the stages of the catechumen's journey to see what each can teach us about the meaning of initiation and thus about the meaning of Christian life. If you are familiar with the catechumenate, the connections will be more obvious to you, but each chapter will highlight some aspect of the RCIA as a basis for our reflections, so it is not necessary to be an expert on the catechumenate to benefit from this book.

The chapters may be used for personal prayer and meditation and/or as the basis for group discussions. Through such reflection and discussion, readers can deepen their own awareness of their identity as the baptized and find new ways to live the new life that God has given us through the sacraments of initiation.

In his *Small Catechism*, Martin Luther suggests that the Christian should daily be drowned by sorrow and repentance and daily come forth and rise from death again. I take this to mean that we should live each day as though we just emerged from the font. It is this image that leads to the title of the book. Each of us is called to live as though we have just come out of the baptismal font, to live the Christian life with the enthusiasm and commitment of those who have just gone into the death of baptism and come out the other side to a new way of life. If these reflections assist the readers in doing that, then they will be a success and God will be glorified in the renewed spirit of our lives.

For Prayer

Father, God of mercy, through these waters of baptism you have filled us with new life as your very own children. Blessed be God.

From all who are baptized in water and the Holy Spirit, you have formed one people, united in your Son, Jesus Christ. Blessed be God.

You have set us free and filled our hearts with the Spirit of your love, that we may live in your peace. Blessed be God.

You call those who have been baptized to announce the Good News of Jesus Christ to people everywhere. Blessed be God (RCIA, no. 222-C).

For Reflection and Discussion

1. How often are you aware that you are a baptized person? What effects does this awareness have when it is present? What triggers it for you?

2. How often do you hear other members of your family or your parish allude to the fact of their baptismal identity? Do you think your parish would benefit if more people were more often conscious of their baptisms?

3. Are infant baptisms celebrated as parish events in your parish? How could these celebrations be enhanced?

4. Has your parish implemented the Rite of Christian Initiation of Adults? How central is it to your parish life?

5. How has the RCIA affected your own understanding of baptism, confirmation, and the Eucharist? How has it affected the parish at large?

2

The Journey of a Lifetime

An atheist was spending a quiet day fishing when suddenly his boat was attacked by the Loch Ness monster. In one easy flip the beast tossed him and his boat high into the air. Then it opened its mouth to swallow both.

As the man sailed head over heels, he cried out, "Oh, my God! Help me!"

At once, the ferocious attack scene froze in place, and as the atheist hung in mid-air, a booming voice came down from the clouds, "I thought you didn't believe in me!"

"Come on, God, give me a break!!" the man pleaded. "Two minutes ago I didn't believe in the Loch Ness monster either!"

How easy life would be if conversion really happened that quickly! In real life, however, conversion is usually a long, slow process. Few of us experience dramatic moments like St. Paul's encounter with the Lord on the road to Damascus. Even that conversion experience required time for Paul to process what had happened to him. For three days he was unable to see, until Ananias laid hands on him and healed him. He stayed with the disciples in Damascus for "some days," according to Acts 9:19, before beginning to proclaim the Gospel. Later passages in Acts and Galatians indicate that it took time for Paul to be accepted in the Christian community and that he grew in his understanding of Jesus over a period of years (see Gal 1:18, for example).

Paul's temporary blindness might remind us of the cure of the blind man recounted in Mark 8:22-26. He was healed of his blindness in stages, and some Scripture scholars see this as an image of the gradual enlightenment of those called to faith in Jesus.

The *Catechism of the Catholic Church* reflects a similar perspective: "The faith required for Baptism is not a perfect and mature faith, but a beginning that is called to develop. . . . For all the baptized, children or adults, faith must grow *after* Baptism" (no. 1253–54).

The Process of Coming to Faith

One of the key words used in describing the Rite of Christian Initiation of Adults is the word "process." The ritual text describes not only the liturgical celebrations around catechumens and candidates for full communion with the Catholic Church, but also the process that leads up to those ritual moments and the process that flows from those celebrations. The rituals only make sense in connection with the process. If the process of conversion and formation that we call the catechumenate does not happen, then the liturgies become empty rituals rather than true celebrations of God's love and grace at work in the lives of the initiates.

As we have learned to link process and celebration in the catechumenate, we are also recovering an awareness that every sacramental celebration also requires a process leading up to it and a process flowing from it. Without these, the sacraments can easily lose their meaning and their power in our lives. They come to be viewed as "magical" moments when God does something instantaneously rather than celebrations of what God is already doing and continues to do in our lives. The RCIA is helping us recover a richer and more realistic view of sacraments and the processes of growth that are intended to accompany these central rituals of our faith.

Process, Not Program

This view of the journey to faith as a process is often distinguished in catechumenate circles from viewing it as a program. A program has a set beginning, clear steps along the way, and a set conclusion. People in a program generally follow the steps as a group, "graduating" from the program at the end.

We are quite used to programs in church life. Our schools and religious education programs generally follow this model. Many other parish activities are also structured as programs, taking groups of people through a series of classes or sessions or projects. We even tend to think of sacramental preparation as a program, since it has often been linked to a school or religious education curriculum.

The Rite of Christian Initiation of Adults is not a program but an ongoing process of conversion. People enter the process when God calls them, and they progress through the process as the Spirit calls them to the next stage. Careful discernment is needed to determine when each person is ready to become a catechumen or to enter the final stage of preparation for the sacraments. This discernment is a process of determining how the Holy Spirit is acting in the person's life and how his or her conversion is progressing under the Spirit's direction. The catechumenate is an ongoing order in the Church, which people enter and leave at their own rate under the guidance of the Holy Spirit.

Life as Process

The pattern of initiation sets the pattern for the whole of Christian life. If the journey to baptism is a flexible process, then

Christian life after baptism is also a process. Growth continues as God constantly calls us to deeper faith and commitment.

Social analysts have noted that contemporary American work lives and careers are becoming more of a process, too. Rather than finding a job or a type of work that is embraced from youth until retirement, many people today find themselves moving from company to company, from job to job, and even into whole new careers. As we become more accustomed to our work life as a "work-in-progress," perhaps it will be easier for us to see our faith life in a similar way.

Because religious formation has been tied so closely in the past to school-year programs, we can easily think of our growth in Christ as a program from which we graduate. Many adult Catholics seem to think that they were finished with religious formation when they left eighth grade or graduated from high school. The journey of faith, however, is a lifelong journey. The Lord continues to call us to growth throughout our lives.

A little boy asked his father, "Daddy, how much does it cost to get married?" The father replied, "I don't know, son, I'm still paying!" What begins at the wedding is lived out in the years that follow, and the marriage relationship continues to develop day by day. In a similar way, what begins in baptism is lived out in the years that follow, and our relationship with the Lord continues to develop throughout our lives.

Being Patient with our Growth

Dealing with a process requires great patience. With a program we know when things will be finished, and we generally have a clearly defined result in mind. Seeing life as a process calls us to more flexibility. As some wise person once put it, "Life is not a problem to be solved but a mystery to be lived." Faith is a journey into mystery, and it does not follow a set program.

Catechumens have to learn to be patient with their rate of growth. Not everyone grows in faith at the same pace.

Some may seem to make rapid progress, while others find growth much slower. There is no deadline. People can (and should) remain as catechumens for as long as they need, until they are ready to take on the responsibility that flows from being baptized.

After baptism, too, our growth in Christ requires patience. We do not all grow at the same rate. If we are striving for a new depth in prayer or struggling to overcome a habit of sin, we can become very impatient with ourselves. We want to see results, and we want them quickly. It reminds me of a little prayer: "Give me patience, O Lord, and give it to me right now!" It takes patience to wait on God's time.

Learning to be patient with our own growth should also make us more patient with others. Sometimes we expect teens, for example, to have a fully developed moral sense before they have had enough life experience to have developed such a finely tuned conscience. Even adults with much life experience only come to maturity in Christ over many years. If God can be patient with us, we can learn to be patient with ourselves and one another.

Discerning the Spirit

The process of growing in faith occurs in response to the action of the Holy Spirit within us. We do not come to faith by our own effort. God always takes the initiative and makes the first move. Our whole spiritual lives consist of our responses to God's initiative.

To respond appropriately, we need to be attentive to the promptings of the Holy Spirit. Sometimes these come to us from outside, as it were, through the people we meet and in the events that happen in our lives. Sometimes the Spirit prompts us from within, enlightening our minds and moving our hearts toward the Lord. In either case, it is often easy to ignore the Spirit's guidance.

Just as catechumens need to develop an awareness of the presence and action of the Spirit in their lives, so those already baptized need to foster a lifelong attentiveness to the guidance of the Spirit.

Ultimately this is what spiritual direction, meditation, and other forms of spiritual discipline are intended to foster. A good spiritual director helps the directee to be more attentive to what the Spirit is saying. Time spent in centering prayer or meditation is intended to quiet the mind and heart enough to hear the voice of the Spirit. The various traditions of spirituality in the Church are all, at root, ways of being more attentive to the promptings of the Spirit.

The role of discernment throughout the catechumenate reminds us of the importance of taking the time and making the effort throughout our lives to discern what the Spirit is saying to us. The gift of the Holy Spirit, which we celebrate in baptism and confirmation, is the greatest gift we receive from God.

Our tradition speaks of this gift as Uncreated Grace. The presence of the Holy Spirit dwelling within us is the source of all the other forms of grace that our tradition distinguishes. The Spirit within makes us holy, and we call that sanctifying grace. The Spirit enables us to act properly day by day, and we call that actual grace. The Spirit draws us further into the divine life when we celebrate the sacraments, and we call that sacramental grace. Attentiveness to the Spirit enables us to make full use of this great gift of God.

A People on Pilgrimage

The Spirit of God calls us forth on the journey of faith and leads us day by day on our pilgrimage. Since the Second Vatican Council, we have become more accustomed to speaking of the Church as a pilgrim people. This community of faith is always on the move. We may pause on our pilgrimage to rest a bit at an oasis in the desert, but if we are tempted to stay in one place too long, the Spirit nudges us (sometimes gently, sometimes more forcefully) and reminds us that "we have here no lasting city."

We never reach a point where we can accurately say that we have finished the journey, at least not this side of heaven. We are pilgrims for life. Like the column of cloud and the pillar of fire leading the Israelites through the wilderness to the promised land, the Spirit goes before us leading us toward the kingdom of God.

Those who study initiation rituals in various cultures often speak of a stage of initiation called liminality, from the Latin word for threshold. In the liminal stage, initiates are betwixt and between. They have left their former way of life or status in the tribe but have not yet come to their new position. This stage is crucial for growth, as the initiates surrender their ties to the past and prepare to enter into a new future.

The catechumenate can be understood as a liminal experience. The catechumens become members of the Church when they celebrate the rite of acceptance into the catechumenate, yet they are not full members until they celebrate the sacraments of initiation. For the period of the catechumenate, they are in a liminal situation.

There is a significant difference between Christian initiation and the standard anthropological model, however. In the standard model, the initiate moves from the liminal period at the end of the initiation and takes his or her place in the structure of the group. The liminal condition is temporary. When catechumens celebrate the sacraments and enter the order of the faithful, they really move from one liminal state to another. Christianity itself is a liminal way of life. We are in the world but not of the world, and we are constantly on pilgrimage. We do not arrive until after this life on earth is ended.

It is not easy to be perpetual pilgrims. We humans have a settling-down instinct that wants to get comfortable and stay put. Those who live their baptism daily may need to remind themselves often that they follow a Christ who had "nowhere to lay his head." The journey of the catechumens continually reminds those already baptized that our God keeps calling us to leave the past behind and "keep on movin' on."

For Prayer

God gives light to everyone who comes into this world; though unseen, he reveals himself through the works of his hand, so that all people may learn to give thanks to their Creator. You have followed God's light and the way of the Gospel now lies open before you. Set your feet firmly on that path and acknowledge the living God, who truly speaks to everyone. Walk in the light of Christ and learn to trust in his wisdom. Commit your lives daily to his care, so that you may come to believe in him with all your heart. This is the way of faith along which Christ will lead you in love toward eternal life (RCIA, 52-A).

For Reflection and Discussion

1. When you hear the word "conversion," what ideas or images does it evoke for you? Do you think of yourself as someone in the process of conversion?

2. Do you understand the distinction between a program and a process of formation? Could you explain to someone else why growth in faith should be seen as a process rather than a program?

3. Can you identify and describe some steps or stages in your own growth in faith? What prompted such growth? What might deepen it in the future?

4. Can you think of times in your life when no growth seemed to be happening? Looking back, can you see growth that occurred during that period but became evident only later in your life?

5. Do you see your own life as an ongoing journey or pilgrimage? Are you aware of the guidance of the Holy Spirit on that journey?

3

Becoming a Christian

A Zen Master from Tibet was visiting New York City. He went up to a hot dog vendor and said, "Make me one with everything."

The hot dog vendor fixed a hot dog and handed it to the Zen Master, who paid with a $20.00 bill. The vendor put the bill in the cash box and closed it.

"Where's my change?" asked the Zen Master.

The vendor responded, "Change must come from within!"

That final line speaks a fundamental truth. Change of mind and heart, true conversion to the Lord, must come from within. One of the most basic truths that those who minister to catechumens and candidates for reception into the Catholic Church must learn (and often recall) is that conversion is the work of the Holy Spirit. None of us can bring about conversion in another person. It is the Spirit of God, working within each person, who brings about conversion to Jesus Christ.

To say that conversion is the work of the Holy Spirit does not mean, however, that it happens automatically or that the person called to conversion does not have to do anything to bring it about. Nor does it mean that other people have no impact on the possibility or the progress of conversion. The work of the Holy Spirit must be welcomed by the person that God invites to conversion. The process is a cooperative one, requiring active cooperation with God's grace, and other people often play a significant role in prompting and supporting that cooperation.

The whole process of the catechumenate is based on the assumption that conversion can be fostered and supported by a community of faith. The Holy Spirit who accomplishes conversion in each individual member of the Church is also given to the church community. The Spirit is the glue that binds the community together, the life force of the Body of Christ that the community forms, and the guiding wisdom that the community strives to embody and to share with those who come to it seeking the Lord. The catechumenate process is designed to encourage and support the work of the Spirit to bring about the initial conversion of those seeking baptism. It recognizes the irreplaceable action of God's grace and also the valuable assistance in the conversion process that can be offered by sponsors, the catechumenate team, and members of the whole faith community.

A Lifelong Journey

The process of becoming Christian can be understood in two ways. The initial process, experienced in the catechumenate, leads a person to the sacraments of initiation. This process makes a person a Christian, a member of the community of faith in Jesus Christ. Such a person has become a Christian.

Yet the journey is not complete once we have been baptized. We spend the rest of our lives trying to grow into our identity as Christians, as members of the Body of Christ, as disciples of the Lord. In this sense, we never finish becoming Christian, at least until we leave this earth. The journey of conversion is an ongoing journey that lasts throughout our lives and perhaps even beyond death. What else is purgatory but the final stage of conversion of our hearts?

The idea that conversion lasts a lifetime is a new idea for many Catholics. We are accustomed to using the term "convert" to refer to those who were not baptized Catholic as infants but joined the Church at some later point. In the broader sense, however, all of us are converts. We are all on a lifetime journey of conversion, seeking to become more and more like Christ, to become truly Christian.

The need for continuing conversion, then, is a hallmark of the Catholic view of the spiritual life. In contrast to those who view conversion as a one-time, "born-again" experience, the Catholic tradition sees it as an ongoing process. While a member of some other Christian denomination might claim, "I am saved," a Catholic might respond, "I am being saved, day by day, by God's grace."

Much of what our tradition has described as means of spiritual growth can be understood as tools for ongoing conversion. Celebration of the Eucharist, frequent confession, daily prayer, nightly examination of conscience, acts of charity and numerous other spiritual "works" are all intended to deepen our conformity to Christ, which is another way to speak of conversion. All of the various schools of spirituality in the Church (Ignatian, Franciscan, Benedictine, etc.) are simply different methods of fostering deeper conversion.

Conversion From and Conversion To

The conversion journey of the catechumenate, then, provides a model for the rest of Christian life. As catechumens are led through a process of initial conversion of mind and heart and life, so those already baptized continue the process of giving themselves more completely to the Lord every day of their lives.

Conversion always involves turning away from sin and turning toward Christ. It requires leaving behind the past in order to move into a better future. It entails letting go of the familiar so that we can grasp more fully onto Christ and the wonders he has in store for us.

It is this necessity of "letting go" that makes conversion difficult for us. We humans seem to have a perverse instinct to hold on to what is familiar and comfortable even when we know that it is not good for us. We prefer the familiar, even if it is painful and ugly, over the new that may be joyful and beautiful.

The only way to be able to let go of the negative is to focus more strongly on the promise of a better future. Christ has repeatedly promised us life and love and all good things if we trust him. Conversion is ultimately about claiming those promises for our own lives.

Living the Paschal Mystery

The surrender that conversion requires sometimes feels like death. We even reflect that in our language: "I'd rather die than have to do that!" This can remind us that conversion to Christ means embracing the paschal mystery, his death and resurrection. The catechumenate comes to a climactic point when the community celebrates the death and resurrection of the Lord each year during the Triduum, the great Three Days from Holy Thursday evening until Easter Sunday evening.

The paschal mystery is a touchstone for the catechumens and candidates long before the Triduum, however. Throughout their formation, they are gradually led to an identification with Christ through a willingness to die to sin so that they might rise to new life. What is celebrated fully at the Easter Vigil, when they enter the waters of the font to die and rise with Christ, has already become a way of life for them.

After their baptism, the paschal mystery continues to be the motif of their lives. All the baptized are continually called to die to sin and selfishness that they might live more fully the new life of the risen Christ.

As we share more and more fully in Christ's dying and rising, we are being conformed more completely to his image. His death and resurrection were not isolated events in his life. They were really the culmination of a life devoted to doing God's will, to putting others before himself, and to giving of himself in love. As we increasingly become "dead to sin and living for God in Christ Jesus" (Rom 6:11), we become more like Christ himself. Step by step we grow into our identity as members of the Body of Christ and are thus increasingly able to make him present in our world.

Conversion as Gift

A man dies and goes to heaven. Of course, St. Peter meets him at the Pearly Gates.

St. Peter says, "Here's how it works. You need one hundred points to make it into heaven. You tell me all the good things you've done, and I give you a certain number of points for each item, depending on how good it was. When you reach one hundred points, you get in."

"Okay," the man says, "I was married to the same woman for fifty years and never cheated on her, even in my heart."

"That's wonderful," says St. Peter, "that's worth three points!"

"Three points?" he says, slightly concerned. "Well, I attended church all my life and supported its ministry with my tithe and service."

"Terrific!" says St. Peter. "That's certainly worth a point."

"One point!?!" he moans, now really getting worried. "I started a soup kitchen in my city and worked in a shelter for homeless veterans."

"Fantastic, that's good for two more points," he says.

"Two points!" the man cries. "At this rate the only way I get into heaven is by the grace of God!"

St. Peter nods and says, "Bingo, one hundred points! Come on in, my son!"

Because turning away from sin and embracing a gospel way of life is often difficult, it is easy for us to begin thinking of conversion as something that we do and salvation as something that we earn. Nothing could be farther from the truth! Salvation is a gift from God that we can never earn. Conversion, too, is really a gift of God. It is God's grace that calls us to conversion, and it is God's grace that enables us to be converted.

Remembering the priority of God's grace will keep us from pride and move us to a life of continual thanksgiving. Thanksgiving should be our constant stance in life, since all that we have comes to us as a gift from God. That is why initiation culminates in the celebration of the Eucharist, the Church's great act of communal thanksgiving. The very word "eucharist" comes from the Greek word for thanksgiving. Through the sacraments of initiation we become a eucharistic people, a people who constantly give thanks.

Accepting the Gift

Any gift we receive is useless, of course, unless it is welcomed and put to use. This is also true of the gift of grace. God freely offers us the gift of new life and the possibility of deep conversion. It is not something that we earn, but it is something that requires our response. In order for the gift to be effective in our lives, we must welcome it and cooperate with the grace God offers us.

At root, this cooperation is a matter of accepting God's will for our lives. Our tendency to sin is fundamentally a willfulness that wants to put our will over God's will. Conversion is a matter of surrender to God's will.

This surrender requires an openness to change. Conversion, obviously, requires change, and yet many Christians seem to think that religion is something that should not require them to change. Change is sometimes treated as a "dirty word" in church circles. If conversion is a lifelong journey for Christians, then faith requires a constant willingness to change. In the often quoted words of Cardinal John Henry Newman, "In a higher world, it is otherwise, but here below, to live is to change, and to be perfect is to have changed often."[1] If we find ourselves resisting change, we may well be resisting God's call to conversion and growth. This is especially true if our resistance arises primarily because we find change uncomfortable or too demanding. Openness to change is perhaps the primary requirement for our continued conversion and continued spiritual growth in Christ.

Conforming our wills to God's will means adopting the values of the Gospel, which often means rejecting the values of the world. Whether we have been raised in the Church or come to it as adults, we are still deeply influenced by the culture in which we live. The values of our society are constantly promoted by the media and by people around us. It takes a constant effort to discern the impact of false values in our thoughts and attitudes and to reject them in favor of gospel values. Conversion is a daily challenge.

Summary

The *Catechism of the Catholic Church* offers us a good summary of the Church's understanding of conversion:

> Jesus calls to conversion. This call is an essential part of the proclamation of the kingdom: "The time is fulfilled, and the kingdom of God is at hand; repent, and believe in the gospel." In the Church's preaching this call is addressed

---

[1] John Henry Cardinal Newman, *An Essay on the Development of Christian Doctrine* (London: Longmans, Green, and Co., 1909) 41.

first to those who do not yet know Christ and his Gospel. Also, Baptism is the principal place for the first and fundamental conversion. It is by faith in the Gospel and by Baptism that one renounces evil and gains salvation, that is, the forgiveness of all sins and the gift of new life.

Christ's call to conversion continues to resound in the lives of Christians. This *second conversion* is an uninterrupted task for the whole Church who, "clasping sinners to her bosom, [is] at once holy and always in need of purification, [and] follows constantly the path of penance and renewal." This endeavor of conversion is not just a human work. It is the movement of a "contrite heart," drawn and moved by grace to respond to the merciful love of God who loved us first (nos. 1427–28).

Those who live their baptism daily embrace conversion as a lifestyle, allowing God to challenge them to further growth at every stage of their lives.

For Prayer

This is eternal life: to know the one true God and Jesus Christ whom he has sent. Christ has been raised from the dead and appointed by God as the Lord of life and ruler of all things, seen and unseen. If, then, you wish to become his disciples and members of his Church, you must be guided to the fullness of truth that he has revealed to us. You must learn to make the mind of Christ your own. You must strive to pattern your life on the teachings of the Gospel and so to love the Lord your God and your neighbor. For this was Christ's command and he was its perfect example (RCIA, no. 52-C).

For Reflection and Discussion

1. As you think of your own growth in your relationship with Christ, how has the parish community assisted you? Are there other people who are not members of the parish who have aided your growth in faith?

2. Beyond a person's initial conversion to Christ, there may be many significant conversion moments in one's life. Can you point to any of those in your own history? Have you recognized such experiences in others?

3. Do you experience the process of conversion in your own life as primarily negative or primarily positive? In what ways has the journey led you to a better life?

4. Do you think of your faith mostly as God's gift or as your response? How often to you thank God for the gift of faith?

5. Do you see the paschal mystery (Christ's death/resurrection) as central to your spiritual life? What makes it difficult for you to surrender to God's will as Jesus did? What helps you to do so?

4

Called into Community

Three men were stranded on a desert island. They had been there a long time, as they had plenty of food and water but no way off the island. One day a big box drifted up to the shore. They excitedly opened the box, only to find a bunch of trash and old rags. At the bottom, though, they found a lamp. Remembering the story of Aladdin, they rubbed the lamp furiously, and lo and behold, a genie appeared. The genie was very glad to be out of the lamp and agreed to grant each of the men any wish he may desire.

The first man said, "You know, I was rich and powerful back at home. I had a multi-million dollar corporation, fast cars, beautiful women. I jet-setted all over the world, eating fine food, drinking fine wine, seeing the world's wonders. My wish is to return to the life I had." POOF!! He disappeared.

The second man said, "Well, I didn't have what that guy has. I just had a job down at the local gas station. But I have a beautiful wife, three wonderful children—a really nice and fulfilling life. My only wish is to return to my home." POOF!! He also disappeared.

Now it was the third man's turn, "Gosh, I didn't have a life at all like either of those two. I'm not rich. I'm not powerful. I'm not married. I'm not anyone's dad. I didn't even have a job or a girlfriend. My life was pathetic. The happiest days of my life were spent right here on this island. You know, my wish is for my two buddies to come back!"

His companions were presumably unhappy with the result, but the third man had figured out the value of community! There are some people who think that they can be good Christians all by themselves on an island. Their faith, they say, is a matter between them and God. Proud of their independence, they claim to need no one else.

The process of formation in the Rite of Christian Initiation of Adults teaches us a very different perspective. One of the most obvious differences between the catechumenate and the private instructions for converts offered before the Second Vatican Council is that the catechumenate is a deeply communal experience. The rite insists that "the initiation of adults is the responsibility of all the baptized" (RCIA, no. 9). The process occurs in the midst of the parish community and relies on the community for a multitude of ministries. One of the four major dimensions of the catechumenate period, for example, is experience of the Christian way of life based on "the example and support of sponsors, godparents and the whole Christian community" (no. 75–2).

The Offer of Salvation

A fundamental assumption of the catechumenate, then, is that initiation and conversion happen in the context of the Christian community. This will not surprise anyone who is familiar with the history of God's dealings with humanity. The Judeo-Christian tradition reveals a God who forms a people. The invitation to liberation and salvation is simultaneously an invitation to become part of God's chosen people. Even when

God calls an individual, the call is to form a people, as when God called Abraham to become the father of a great nation.

The realization that faith is radically communal is a difficult one for many American Catholics. Our culture has been strongly individualistic. We pride ourselves on our ability to lift ourselves up "by our own bootstraps." Our heroic icons are often solo figures, such as the Lone Ranger or James Bond. We cherish our independence and our rights as individuals. We especially value our freedom to choose for ourselves, and it is easy to think of one's choice of religion as a personal, individual matter.

We may even *experience* the decision to seek baptism or join a church as a personal choice, yet the Christian tradition insists that even this choice is a response to God's initiative. And God calls each of us into community.

God's decision in this matter is really a reflection of the way God made human beings. Despite our sometime fascination with radical individualism, we are created with a deep need for human community. We are made to be in relationships, and we grow and become our true selves as a result of significant relationships in our lives. As Genesis put it, "It is not good for the man to be alone" (Gen 2:18).

As true as this is about our basic human needs, it is even more critical in the area of faith. Faith is a communal reality. The *Catechism of the Catholic Church* puts it this way:

> Faith is a personal act—the free response of the human person to the initiative of God who reveals himself. But faith is not an isolated act. No one can believe alone, just as no one can live alone. You have not given yourself faith as you have not given yourself life. The believer has received faith from others and should hand it on to others. Our love for Jesus and for our neighbor impels us to speak to others about our faith. Each believer is thus a link in the great chain of believers. I cannot believe without being carried by the faith of others, and by my faith I help support others in the faith (no. 166).

Part of the Body

The identity of the baptized as members of a community is heightened in the Christian tradition by the image of the Body of Christ. St. Paul insists that we are baptized into one body. "For as in one body we have many parts, and all the parts do not have the same function, so we, though many, are one body in Christ and individually parts of one another" (Rom 12:4; see also 1 Cor 10:17; 12:12-20, and Eph 5:30).

Being part of one body and "individually parts of one another" may seem a very strange idea to many Americans because of our hyper-individualistic culture, but it is basic to a proper understanding of our identity as Christians. We are not just a loose association of like-minded individuals. We are part of Christ's body and thus intimately linked to one another.

The experience of the catechumenate helps the initiates to grow into their identity as part of a community of faith. They share much of their lives in the process, getting to know one another and members of the parish in the precatechumenate, sharing discussions of the Word of God at their weekly Sunday dismissal sessions and at the catechetical sessions during the catechumenate period, struggling together for deeper conversion during the period of purification and enlightenment, sharing the intense joy of the Easter Vigil, and spending time after Easter sharing what it all meant to them.

It can take a while for some catechumens to become comfortable sharing their faith and their lives, but many also find a need after their baptisms to continue in some kind of faith-sharing group. Once they have experienced the power of a shared faith, it is hard to go back to an individualistic approach.

It also may take a while for many of those baptized as infants to grow into a deep awareness of their identity as parts of the Body of Christ. Becoming part of some group that shares faith is, of course, a great help. This may be a prayer group, a group formed as a small Christian community, or a group dedicated to a specific form of Christian service. Such small groups enable a deeper sharing than is possible in the larger parish setting. Even when we are alone, however, we are still part of the body. Whenever we pray, we pray as part of the body, and it is good to recall that fact at the beginning of our prayer time.

Beyond prayer, our whole life as Christians is shaped by our identity as part of the body. In his book *The Heart of the Enlightened*, Anthony de Mello recounts this fable:

> Once upon a time the members of the body were very annoyed with the stomach. They were resentful that they had to procure food and bring it to the stomach while the stomach itself did nothing but devour the fruit of their labor. So they decided that they would no longer bring the stomach food. The hands would not lift it to the mouth. The teeth would not chew it. The throat would not swallow it. That would force the stomach to do something. But all they succeeded in doing was to make the body weak to the point that they were all threatened with death. So it was finally they who learned the lesson that in helping one another they were really working for their own welfare.[1]

Recognizing ourselves as part of one body prompts us to work together for the common good, not only in the Church but in our society as well. Christian morality flows from Christian identity; it is a call to be who we are, to recognize our common identity and to act accordingly.

Recognizing Christ

Being part of the body shapes our response to other members of the body. An oft-told tale tells of a guru who asked his

---

[1] Anthony de Mello. *The Heart of the Enlightened* (New York: Doubleday, 1989) 133.

disciples how they could tell when the night had ended and the day had begun:

> One answered, "When you see an animal in the distance and can tell whether it is a cow or horse."
>
> "No," said the guru.
>
> Another offered: "When you look at a tree in the distance and can tell if it is an oak tree or a maple tree."
>
> "Wrong again," said the guru. "Unless you can look into the face of any man and recognize your brother and look in the face of any woman and recognize your sister, it is still night."

Christians go even beyond this wise advice, seeing in the face of their brothers and sisters the face of Christ himself. Mother Teresa, when asked how she was able to keep ministering to the dying beggars in the streets of Calcutta, answered simply, "I see in them the face of Christ." This was, I believe, the secret to her sanctity. Her life was devoted to serving Christ, and she found him everywhere. As she often pointed out, Christ is not found only in those the world considers poor, for even the very rich often suffer a great poverty of love. Christ may be found in every person we meet.

The poet Adrienne Rich has said that violence is a failure of the imagination. One way to understand that line is that people turn to violence when they fail to imagine better ways of resolving problems. We might also understand it on a deeper level, though. If we use the power of our imagination to see the face of Christ in others, how could we commit violence against them? Violence, hatred, and apathy toward others all indicate a failure of the Christian imagination.

Developing an ability to see the face of Christ in all the people around us could be the key to a rich and full spiritual life. We may never reach the point where this becomes second nature, but trying to see Christ in others a bit more each day sounds like a good recipe for holiness.

This principle is also basic to our understanding of a basic tenet of our faith—the incarnation. This doctrine refers first to the fact that God took on human flesh in Jesus Christ. God became incarnate (which means enfleshed) in Jesus, but the mystery of the Incarnation continues after the Resurrection because Christ now dwells in all the members of his body, the Church. God continues to be bodily present in our world through the community of faith, and it is this presence in the Church that undergirds and is the reason for his bodily presence in the Eucharist. He gives himself to us bodily in the sacrament to sustain his presence in us who are his body.

All who are baptized are called, therefore, not only to see Christ in others but also to reveal Christ to others. We have become part of his body so that we can make him present to our world. Paradoxically, the best way we can make sure that others can see Christ in us is for us to see him in them. If we treat others as we treat Christ, then they will see him in us. We may never know that this has happened. If we find out, it may be years later when people tell us the effect of our ministry to them. It is probably better that way, for if we knew when Christ was revealing himself through us we might be tempted by pride, which would then block others from seeing the Lord in us.

Those who are baptized after a rich experience of the catechumenate know that their faith is linked to the community that welcomes them. Those who live their baptism daily reflect often on their identity as members of the Body of Christ, remembering that they are called to make him present wherever they go and to look for his face in everyone they meet.

For Prayer

These catechumens, who are our brothers and sisters, have already traveled a long road. We rejoice with them in the gentle guidance of God who has brought them to this day. Let us pray that they may press onwards, until they come to share fully in our way of life; that God our Father may reveal Christ to them more and more with every passing day; that they may undertake with generous hearts and souls whatever God may ask of them; that they may have our sincere and unfailing support every step of the way; that they may find in our community compelling signs of unity and generous love; that their hearts and ours may become more responsive to the needs of others (RCIA, no. 65).

For Reflection and Discussion

1. How many different communities can you name of which you are a part? Can you express how each of them shapes your own identity?

2. In what ways, positive or negative, has the church community shaped your life? How could the Church be a more positive force for you?

3. How often do you think of yourself as a part of the Body of Christ? Is that a helpful image for you? Why or why not?

4. What influence might a heightened sense of being part of the Body of Christ have on your daily actions?

5. Do you find it easy or difficult to recognize the face of Christ in others? Can you think of ways to make such recognition more frequent in your life?

5

Welcoming the Stranger

The first stage in the catechumenal process is called the precatechumenate. It is a time of inquiry and welcome. Inquirers come seeking to learn about the Church and its faith. The Church invites them in and welcomes their questions and concerns. One of the goals of the parish is to get to know them and their background.

> The Smiths were proud of their family tradition. Their ancestors had come to America on the Mayflower. They had included U. S. senators and Wall Street wizards. They decided to compile a family history, a legacy for their children and grandchildren, so they hired a fine author. Only one problem arose—how to handle that great-uncle George, who was executed in the electric chair. The author said he could handle the story tactfully. When the book appeared, it said that "Great-uncle George occupied a chair of applied electronics at an important government institution; he was attached to his position by the strongest of ties, and his death came as a great shock."

Sharing Stories

One of the primary things that happens in the precatechumenate is the telling of stories. Though their family histories may not be as colorful as the Smiths', the seekers are invited to share the story of their lives and their families and thus to begin to reveal where God has been at work in their personal histories. The church community shares its story, too. Members of the community share their own faith stories as well as stories of the local parish.

The most important story that the Church offers, however, is the story of God's actions among us through the centuries. This story is recorded primarily in the Bible, the story book of the community of faith. Thus this time of inquiry is also described in the Rite of Christian Initiation of Adults as a time of evangelization.

Evangelization is not really a process of beating people over the head with biblical texts. Effective evangelization does not try to give people answers to questions they have not yet asked. Remember the old bumper sticker: "Jesus is the answer. What is the question?"

Good evangelization means listening to the stories and questions that people share and then responding to them with whatever the Scriptures offer us that relates to their issues. An example may help to clarify the process. When a group of catechumens was upset about the fact that the already baptized and catechized candidates for full communion did not have to spend as long in preparation for the sacraments as the catechumens did, the catechumenate director might well have shared with them the parable of the workers in the vineyard. This parable about workers who got the same pay whether they had worked one hour or the whole day speaks rather directly to their concerns about fairness. In the parable Jesus responded to similar concerns by reminding us that grace is God's gift. It is not something that can be earned but can only be welcomed with gratitude.

This process of linking our personal stories and concerns with the Scriptures continues throughout the whole of the catechumenate process, which is a good indication that it should also continue throughout our lives after baptism. As Christians, we are to be a biblical people, a people who know the Bible well from regular reading, study, and prayer and who know how to apply the biblical message to the events of daily life. Whenever we face difficult decisions or have questions about the meaning of events in our lives, we should instinctively turn to the wisdom distilled in the Sacred Scriptures for guidance and understanding.

The sharing of stories in the process of initiation is not just a matter of speaking the narratives. Once stories are spoken, they need to interact. In the end, the goal is that our personal stories are integrated into the story of salvation. The core of that story, of course, is the story of the life, death, and resurrection of Jesus Christ. The Church responds to initiates' stories with the good news of Jesus Christ in the hope that they will find that good news persuasive. They are invited to try out the story of Jesus as a way to interpret the meaning of their own experience. If they find that the story makes sense, they will be likely to make Christ's story their own, to shape their future in line with the values and example of Jesus.

A Community of Welcome

Sharing stories of one's life and faith is a significant act of welcome. To share on such deep levels makes one vulnerable, and inviting another to enter into that space is powerful hospitality. The inquirer who approaches the Church is invited to risk such vulnerability, but that is only likely to happen if those who represent the Church take the risk first. Vulnerability invites vulnerability because it dismantles defenses.

The community of the Church must be such a place of welcome. The mission that Jesus entrusted to the Church requires a constant reaching out, a continual openness, a perpetual stance of invitation to the stranger to come and see. Such openness is a challenge for any community, just as it is for any individual. It means resisting the natural tendency to put up walls, to circumscribe limits, and to stay with those with whom we are already comfortable. The Christian community must strive to be as open as the Lord himself, ready to welcome sinners and strangers of every kind.

Welcoming the stranger has been recognized as an important virtue since Old Testament times. The Israelites are commanded, as part of the offering of first fruits, to say, "My father was a wandering Aramean who went down to Egypt with a small household and lived there as an alien" (Deut 26:5). Remembering their own history is intended to shape their behavior, as God made clear in the rules he gave Moses: "You shall not oppress an alien; you well know how it feels to be an alien, since you were once aliens yourselves in the land of Egypt" (Exod 23:9).

In the New Testament, the Letter to the Hebrews gives an additional reason for hospitality: "Do not neglect hospitality, for through it some have unknowingly entertained angels" (Heb 13:2). This reference to Abraham and Sarah's welcome of strangers (one of whom turns out to be God who promises them a son) reminds us that strangers often bring blessings to those who welcome them.

The catechumens' experience of such welcome invites them to grow into people of hospitality, too. After their baptism, they will be expected to embrace a similar openness toward others who seek the Lord, inviting them to come and see what the Church has to offer.

An Open Heart

This openness must go beyond church activities, though. The church community will only be hospitable if it is made up of people who have adopted hospitality as a lifestyle. This is not primarily a matter of offering coffee and cookies (though it may include that!) but of striving to live with an open heart.

This challenge can shape a whole spirituality, for opening our heart to other people is closely linked with opening our heart to the Lord. Both require us to lower our defenses, to risk encounter, and often to go beyond our comfort zones.

Many times God comes to us in the guise of the stranger. Leo Tolstoy's famous story about Martin the cobbler ("Where Love Is, There is God Also") tells of the shoemaker who spent a whole day waiting for the Lord, who had promised to visit him. In the course of the day, he welcomed and aided an old man who had been shoveling snow, a poor woman with her baby, and a hungry young boy caught stealing an apple from an old woman on the street. When the day is over, all these people appear to him as apparitions who identify themselves as the Lord who had visited him. The story concludes with the words of Matthew's Gospel, "Whatever you did for one of these least brothers of mine, you did for me."

This point is so basic to Christian life, yet we so often forget it. We are like the man who was lost in the desert. Later when describing his ordeal to his friends, he told how in sheer despair he had knelt down and cried out to God to help him. "And did God answer your prayer?" he was asked. "Oh no! Before he could, an explorer appeared and showed me the way." Like this man, we can easily forget that God usually acts in our lives through other people and wants to act in others' lives through us.

The reason we resist such openness to God and to others, of course, is that they keep making demands on us. Those demands are really gifts, for they invite us to deeper conversion and thus to fuller life in Christ. The call, as always, is a call to embrace the cross. We are called to die to self in order to live for others, and that call involves surrendering our defenses and our comfort. The promise hidden in the call is the promise that the cross always leads to new life. Our defenses always seem to us to protect and ensure our life, but they frequently prevent us from living more fully. God's call to transcend them is always a call to live more fully and more richly. "I came," Jesus said, "so that they may have life and have it more abundantly" (John 10:10).

This challenge to be open links prayer and action in Christian life. Openness to God is basic to true prayer. Prayer is less about getting God to do what we want than getting ourselves in tune with what God wants. Then God can do great things for us and through us, and the most basic wonder God brings about in us is the ability to love. As Jesus noted in speaking of the greatest commandment, love of God and love of neighbor are intimately linked. If we are truly open to God and allow God's love to fill us, then we also allow God's love to flow through us to others. Openness to others, then, is a good indication of how open we are to God.

Because our God is a God whose love embraces all people, openness to God's will requires us to be open to all people, regardless of their race, language, ethnic identity, gender, economic status, sexual orientation, or any other criteria that society uses to distinguish and divide people.

This is a challenge for the church community as a whole. It is easier and more comfortable to worship with and interact with only "our own kind," however that may be defined. A church that claims to follow Jesus Christ, however, must be willing to embrace all those for whom he gave his life. The Church must constantly strive to be "catholic," that is, universal. It includes people of every nation and race and culture, and local parishes must also be willing to embrace people from many different backgrounds. Many parishes in the United States are discovering the need to function with a more multi-cultural approach in order to respond to the spiritual needs of all those who live in their area. Immigration patterns and changing demographics are one way that God is calling us to greater openness.

What is true for the parish is also true for each member. When God brings people into our life who are different from us, God is calling us to open our hearts more widely and broaden the circle of those we recognize as brothers and sisters. Widening the circle of our love is not a bad description of all spiritual growth. Shaped by the Word of God, those who live their baptism daily are constantly striving to widen their circle to embrace all those who are loved by the Lord they claim to follow.

For Prayer

Father of mercy, we thank you for these your servants. You have sought and summoned them in many ways and they have turned to seek you. You have called them today and they have answered in our presence. We praise you, Lord, and we bless you (RCIA, no. 53).

Almighty God, source of all creation, you have made us in your image. Welcome with love those who come before you today. They have listened among us to the word of Christ; by its power renew them and by your grace refashion them, so that in time they may assume the full likeness of Christ, who lives and reigns for ever and ever. Amen (RCIA, no. 66-B).

For Reflection and Discussion

1. Reviewing your own life, what significant experiences can you name that shaped your spiritual life?

2. What kinds of experiences have made you most aware of God's presence in your life?

3. What reactions does the word "evangelization" evoke in you? Can you name experiences when you have evangelized others, by word or action?

4. Would you describe your parish community as a very welcoming church? What could help it become more hospitable to those who come seeking a church to call home?

5. How open is your own heart? Do you find it easy or difficult to let newcomers and new ideas into your life? Can you explain why it is easy or difficult for you?

6

Echoing the Word

A concerned husband went to a doctor to talk about his wife. He said, "Doc, I think my wife is deaf because she never hears me the first time, and I always have to repeat things."

"Well," the doctor replied, "go home tonight, and while she's at the stove cooking, stand about fifteen feet from her and say something to her. If she doesn't reply, move about five feet closer and say it again. Keep moving closer until she hears you. That will give you a good idea of the severity of her deafness."

So, the husband went home and did exactly as instructed. About fifteen feet from his wife in the kitchen, where she was chopping some vegetables, he said, "Honey, what's for dinner?" He heard no response. He moved about five feet closer and asked again. No reply. He moved five feet closer. Still no reply. So he moved right behind her and asked again, "Honey, what's for dinner?"

She replied, "For the fourth time, beef stew!"

Learning to Hear

Listening is a basic dynamic of the catechumenate. The word "catechize" comes from Greek words that mean to echo or resound. A catechumen is thus one who learns to echo the word of God in his or her life. For that to happen, of course, the catechumen must first learn to listen to the word of the Lord. The hearing of the Word of God is central to the period of the process called the Catechumenate Period.

Thus the rite of Acceptance into the Order of Catechumens begins with the inquirers' first formal "acceptance of the Gospel." Those seeking to be catechumens commit themselves to travel on the "way of the Gospel," and their sponsors and the community agree to help them on their journey. Later in the ritual, after they have heard the Word of God proclaimed and preached, they may also be presented with a Bible or with the Lectionary as a reminder that they are to carry this word with them through their lives.

This ritual step of the catechumenate reminds us again of the centrality of the Word of God in our lives. Just as the catechumens commit themselves to live by that word, all the baptized must have frequent recourse to the Word of God if they are to remain faithful to the way of Christ. The Catholic tradition does not see the Bible as the only source of truth and wisdom, but it does see it is an essential source.

All through the catechumenate period, the catechumens will be instructed in the faith of the Church on the basis of the Word of God that is proclaimed each Sunday. They share the Liturgy of the Word with the whole assembly and then leave the full assembly to continue breaking open that word together. Their catechetical session is also built on the word they have heard, for all our doctrine flows from the Scriptures in one way or another. It is God's word that calls them to faith and God's word that forms them in faith.

Those already baptized can take their cue from this pattern, too. More and more parishes are linking their catechesis of children and adults to the Word of God that is proclaimed on Sunday. This offers the opportunity to integrate parish life more fully, so that the whole parish, children and adults, unbaptized and baptized, are formed by the same Word of God week by week. Each member of the assembly can develop a strong spiritual life simply by listening carefully to the word proclaimed on Sunday and carrying that word through the week as a basis for prayer and reflection and daily living.

Like the catechumens, the baptized need to learn how to listen to the Word of God when it is proclaimed at Mass. The first step for many is to stop trying to read the text in a missal or missalette while the word is being proclaimed. It is proclaimed aloud precisely so we can hear the word rather than read it. Active listening is not a skill that our culture encourages, so many people need to learn how to listen well.

The second step is to realize that the goal of this attentive listening is not necessarily to "get it all," to grasp every word and idea in all the readings and the homily. There is too much there for most of us to achieve that, so expecting that of ourselves only leads to frustration. What is important is that we hear the word of the Lord that Christ wants each of us to hear that day. The Holy Spirit enables each of us to hear the word we need to hear. That's the word we need to take with us. The Introduction to the *Lectionary* puts it this way: "The working of the Holy Spirit precedes, accompanies, and brings to completion the whole celebration of the liturgy. But the Spirit also brings home to each person individually everything that in the proclamation of the word of God is spoken for the good of the whole gathering of the faithful" (no. 9).

If we take home one word or idea from the liturgy, then we can return to that message in prayer each day throughout the week. We can strive on a daily basis to put it into practice in our lives. Week by week, day by day, we allow the word that Christ addresses to us to gradually transform us.

Marked with the Cross

There was a priest who went out hunting one day. As he was walking through the woods, he came around a bend and suddenly there was a bear right in the path. The priest took off running as fast as he could, but he slipped and slid down a slope. The bear came right after him. The priest was lying there, and he'd lost his gun, and the bear was coming closer. So the priest said, "Lord, I repent for all my sins. Lord, just please make this bear a Christian." The bear came to a stop, made the sign of the cross and said, "Bless us, O Lord, and these thy gifts which we are about to receive."

Sometimes we make the sign of the cross with about as much meaning as that bear, but during the Rite of Acceptance into the Order of Catechumens, the signing with the cross is a significant ritual symbol. After they commit themselves to follow the Gospel, the catechumens and the candidates are signed with the cross on their foreheads, ears, eyes, lips, heart, shoulders, hands, and feet. The ritual speaks loudly even without words—this person belongs to Christ. Like newly discovered land claimed in the name of the king, this person is claimed in the name of Christ crucified.

The words that accompany the ritual offer further specification and might well be used periodically to challenge ourselves on how well we reflect Christ in our lives. The catechumens receive the sign of the cross on their foreheads as a sign of Christ's love for them. Then they are signed on their ears that they "may hear the voice of the Lord," on their eyes that they "may see the glory of God," and on their lips that they "may respond to the Word of God." They are signed over their hearts that "Christ may dwell there by faith," on their shoulders that they "may bear the gentle yoke of Christ," on their hands that "Christ may be known in the work" that they do, and on their feet that they "may walk in the way of Christ" (RCIA, no. 56).

Those prayers would make a good "morning offering" as we begin each day. What if we signed ourselves every morning on each part of our bodies, consecrating ourselves to the Lord for that day and challenging ourselves to walk in the way of

Christ and to make Christ known in whatever we do that day? Simply signing ourselves, even in silence, can remind us that we are claimed by Christ and that we are to bear the cross with him every day.

The Four Pillars

As the catechumens move through the catechumenate period, they are formed by four fundamental aspects of Christian life (cf. RCIA, no. 75). These four modes of formation might be termed the pillars of the catechumenate period: catechesis, community interaction, prayer and worship, and apostolic service.

The catechumens are given catechesis that is "gradual and complete" and accommodated to the liturgical year. This catechesis is to lead to an "appropriate acquaintance with dogmas and precepts" as well as to "a profound sense of the mystery of salvation."

They are also to become familiar with the Christian way of life, guided by "the example and support of sponsors, godparents, and the entire Christian community." Their integration into the Christian community is a primary way that they learn to follow Christ and to live the faith.

They learn to pray and celebrate with the Church, both by taking part in parish worship and by special times of prayer and celebration arranged for them.

They share in the apostolic work of the Church, working to "spread the Gospel and build up the Church" along with other members of the community.

All four of these aspects of Christian formation are essential to the catechumenate, and good catechumenate teams strive for a balance among them to ensure a solid formation for the initiates. These same four pillars should also form the ongoing life of those already baptized.

Each of us needs ongoing catechesis that not only helps us to understand the dogmas and precepts of the church but also guides us deeper into the mystery at the heart of our faith. This might happen in formal classes or faith sharing groups, or it might happen through reading Catholic books, magazines, and newspapers. Each baptized member of the Church has a responsibility to continue to deepen his or her understanding and appreciation of the faith.

We all need regular contact and interaction with the community of faith, both gaining from and offering support to each other as we share the mission Christ has entrusted to us. Each of us needs to take the time and make the effort to reach out to other members of the parish and to foster the bonds of unity that make us one body in Christ.

Each of us needs a variety of forms of prayer, both individual and communal. Church law requires our participation in the Sunday Eucharist, but we all need other forms of communal prayer and other times for individual prayer as well. Personal prayer should be a daily habit, and we should also take advantage of various opportunities to share prayer and worship with other members of the community.

We are called to reach out to others in service, making the love of God real to people and inviting them to share our faith. This is the responsibility of all the baptized, not just of those ordained to special ministries in the Church. Some of this will occur in parish-based groups, but much of it needs to happen wherever we live and work. Christian service is not just a requirement for confirmation or something for youth groups to undertake. It should be the basic lifestyle of every member of the faith community.

As with the catechumens, it is important for each of us to find some balance among these four pillars. It is easy to focus on one or two and ignore the others. Some people are very strong on prayer and worship, for example, but have no time for study or service—their worship may soon become empty ritual. Others might be very committed to social action or charitable works but find little time for prayer—their service may become politics or humanism rather than the ministry of Christ. Some may be very active in parish life but make little effort to broaden their Christian education—their efforts may become misguided and out of touch with church teaching and theology. Each aspect of Christian life is important, and all of us must find ways to include them all in our lives.

Marked by the cross and formed by the Word of God, those who live their baptism daily seek to maintain a healthy balance of catechesis, community life, prayer, and service as they walk in the way of the Lord and carry on his work in our own time.

For Prayer

Receive the sign of the cross on your forehead. It is Christ himself who now strengthens you with this sign of his love. Learn to know and follow him.

Receive the sign of the cross on your ears, that you may hear the voice of the Lord.

Receive the sign of the cross on your eyes, that you may see the glory of God.

Receive the sign of the cross on your lips, that you may respond to the word of God.

Receive the sign of the cross over your heart, that Christ may dwell there by faith.

Receive the sign of the cross on your shoulders, that you may bear the gentle yoke of Christ.

Receive the sign of the cross on your hands, that Christ may be known in the work which you do.

Receive the sign of the cross on your feet, that you may walk in the way of Christ (RCIA, nos. 55–56).

For Reflection and Discussion

1. Do you find it easy to listen attentively to a friend? Is it more difficult to listen attentively to God's word at Mass? What helps you to listen well, and what makes it difficult for you?

2. How often do you read the Scriptures at home? How do you decide what part of the Bible to read? What benefits have you derived from such use of the Scriptures?

3. Do you prepare for Mass by prayerful reading of the assigned Scriptures for that day? Does your parish publish the citations of the readings in the bulletin so that you can look them up?

4. What do you hope to gain from the Liturgy of the Word at Mass? How often does that happen?

5. How do you begin your day? Do you make some kind of "morning offering"? Do you sign yourself with the cross?

6. Can you describe four activities in your parish that match the four pillars of the catechumenate? In how many of them have you taken part?

7

Called and Chosen

Little Tommy was in the midst of his first day in the first grade. At lunch time, he began to pack up his things to go home. His teacher stopped him and said, "It's time for lunch, Tommy. Why aren't you with the other children?"

Tommy said, "I always go home at lunch. I'll be back tomorrow."

The teacher realized what was going on and said, "That was last year, Tommy, when you were in kindergarten. This year you stay all day. You get to go to lunch, and then you come back to this room to study and do more work. You're only half way through the day . . . there's a lot more."

Tommy thought about that for a moment, then shook his head in frustration and asked, "Who signed me up for that?"

Enrolled for Life

It was presumably his parents who enrolled Tommy for first grade. It is more difficult to answer the question: "Who enrolls catechumens for the celebration of the sacraments?"

This enrollment involves, of course, a decision on the part of the catechumen. We have moved beyond the practice common centuries ago when all the members of a tribe or a territory were baptized because their king or leader decided that they would be Christians. Now a personal decision is required of adults seeking baptism.

The actual enrollment of names for baptism is part of the Rite of Election, generally celebrated on the First Sunday of Lent in the presence of the bishop. The rite notes that the actual inscription of names in the Book of the Elect may be done by the catechumens or by their sponsors or by another minister. More commonly, the names are actually inscribed at the parish earlier in the day during the Rite of Sending of the Catechumens for Election. The Book of the Elect is then presented when the bishop invites the catechumens to enroll their names.

However it happens, this enrollment of names is a significant moment in the catechumens' journey. It signifies their acceptance of the responsibilities that will flow from being baptized. They will never need to ask, "Who signed me up for that?"

What follows the actual inscription or presentation of names is even more significant, however. The bishop formally chooses them for the sacraments and declares them to be "members of the elect." When we elect someone in the political process, we choose them for a certain office. The Rite of Election is also a rite of choosing. The Church, acting through the bishop, chooses these catechumens for the sacraments at the coming Easter Vigil.

The words the bishop says after the formal election remind us, however, that the choice is not ultimately the province of the catechumen or the Church: "God is always faithful to those he calls: now it is your duty, as it is ours, both to be faithful to him in return and to strive courageously to reach the fullness of truth, which your election opens up before you" (RCIA, no. 133). It is God who chooses. It is God who calls us to baptism. The decision of the catechumen and of the Church is really a response to God's call.

A Chosen People

All of those who are baptized, then, are people who have been chosen by God. This fundamental fact carries vast implications. We might spend much of our lives simply reflecting on what it means that God has chosen us as God's special people.

Certainly this awareness of being chosen can be a source of great comfort and strength when life is difficult. Much of the pain we experience in life is a result of rejection. We may feel rejected by one or both of our parents because we could never seem to measure up. We may have been rejected by classmates when they were choosing teams for sports or when they were forming their friendship cliques. We may have been rejected by potential mates who did not return our love. We may feel rejected by people whose friendship we cherished but who did not return our affection. We may have been rejected for a job or a promotion at work. We may have lost a political race. We may feel rejected by our children when they make life choices we do not understand.

No matter how many rejections we may have to endure in life, we can always rely on the basic truth that we have been chosen by God. No matter what else life hands us, we know that God has loved us and chosen us as God's own.

We would probably all do well to spend some time on a regular basis simply meditating on this gift of God. We were not chosen by God because we had achieved great accomplishments. We were not chosen because of our great intelligence. We were not chosen because of our good looks or charming wit. We were not chosen because of our family connections. We were not chosen because of anything we have done or not done. We were chosen because God loves us!

Is there anything more important or more wonderful than to know that we are loved? Is there any more uplifting feeling than knowing that we are special in someone's eyes? Is there any love greater than God's love for us?

No matter what trials we may face in life, we can always rely on that love. When life gets tough, we would do well to remind ourselves: "We are baptized. We are chosen by God. We are loved by the creator of the universe." As St. Paul put it in his Letter to the Romans: "If God is for us, who can be against us? . . . For I am convinced that neither death, nor life, nor angels, nor principalities, nor present things, nor future things, nor powers, nor height, nor depth, nor any other creature will be able to separate us from the love of God in Christ Jesus our Lord" (Rom 8:31, 38-39).

Purification and Enlightenment

The Rite of Election marks the beginning of the third period of the catechumenal process, a period called Purification and Enlightenment. It coincides with Lent and is intended as a time of intense spiritual preparation for the celebration of the Easter sacraments.

This period, like the whole catechumenate, is a response to God's call. It relies on the love of God that was expressed in God's call to baptism. It is a time for the elect to deepen their conversion by allowing God to purify their hearts and enlighten their minds.

The period is marked by the celebration of three scrutinies on the Third, Fourth, and Fifth Sundays of Lent. These rituals are times of prayer for the power of God to be at work in the lives of the elect. The lives of the elect are "scrutinized" or examined, not by the community but by God and by themselves. The rituals are aimed at uncovering and then healing "all that is weak, defective, or sinful in the hearts of the elect" and at bringing out and strengthening "all that is upright, strong, and good" (RCIA, no. 141).

Ongoing Conversion

There are lessons here for those who are already baptized, too. Though the catechumens have been on a conversion journey for months or years already, they still have more growing to do. That is also true for the rest of us.

> Little Johnny watched, fascinated, as his mother smoothed cold cream on her face. "Why do you do that, Mommy?" he asked.
> "To make myself beautiful," said his mother, who then began removing the cream with a tissue.
> "What's the matter?" asked Johnny. "Giving up?"

We can never give up or stop traveling on the road of conversion. It is a natural temptation to want to reach a point where no more change or growth is required of us. In this earthly life, however, that point is never reached. There is always room for improvement. As the catechumens celebrate the scrutinies, they call all of us to deepen our own conversion.

This is really the core dynamic of Lent, for the origins of this season lie in the community's support of those preparing for baptism. As those already baptized prayed and fasted for the elect, they also prepared to renew their own baptismal commitment. For all members of the Church, Lent is a time for intense spiritual growth leading to the celebration of baptism and the renewal of baptismal promises at Easter.

The need for continued conversion is not limited to Lent, of course. Throughout the year and throughout our lives, God constantly calls us to turn away from sin and embrace more fully the gospel way of life.

The Sacrament of Penance

A basic help to this process of ongoing conversion for the already baptized is the sacrament of penance or reconciliation. Ancient writers spoke of penance as a "second baptism" because its goal is to renew our baptismal commitment and restore to us the freedom from sin we first experienced through baptism.

This baptismal connection means that the sacrament of penance finds its premier place during Lent. This is the primary season of the year that we focus in a public and communal way on the call to continuing conversion. That is why most parishes schedule parish penance services and additional times for individual confessions during Lent.

The need for conversion is not limited to any season, however, so this sacrament may be a useful aid to deepening our baptismal commitment at other times as well. Whenever we make use of this sacrament, it is helpful to remember its link to baptism. Baptism is the primary sacrament for the forgiveness of sin; penance finds its meaning as a renewal of that first sacrament.

The use of this sacrament calls for us to scrutinize our lives, much as the elect are called to do for the Lenten scrutinies. We, too, need to uncover whatever is "weak, defective, and sinful" so that God's grace can heal it. We also should bring out what is "upright, strong, and good" so that it might be strengthened. If we are confessing our sins in the individual form of the sacrament, it is good to share both the bad and the good in our lives with the confessor, so that he has a good picture of our spiritual state. In the communal form of the rite during a penance service there may not be time for sharing that completely, but it is still important for us to look at both sides. Some people tend to avoid this sacrament because their experience of it has been unremittingly negative. While its primary focus is the forgiveness of sin, it is helpful to see the sacrament as a means to foster conversion and ongoing growth in our relationship with the Lord. Strengthening the positive is as important as eliminating the negative.

The Rite of Christian Initiation of Adults notes that through the scrutinies "the elect are instructed gradually about the mystery of sin" (no. 143). Some commentators have suggested that the three scrutinies focus on different aspects of sin. The first scrutiny, based on Jesus' meeting with the woman at the well, focuses on personal, individual sin. The second scrutiny, based on the gospel of the man born blind, calls attention to social sins such as treatment of the disabled. The third scrutiny, based on the raising of Lazarus, focuses on sin that leads to death.

The exact focus of each scrutiny could be debated, but the goal of being instructed about the mystery of sin is clear. Many of us baptized years ago may also need to broaden our awareness of sin beyond the purely personal arena. Sin affects the structures of our society and the patterns of our lives. Spiritual growth should lead us into an ever deeper awareness of sin in all its guises so that we can work to overcome it both in our personal lives and in our society.

The celebration of the scrutinies three Sundays in a row might also remind us that the struggle against evil is a constant one. We need to examine our lives on a regular basis if we are to continue to grow in holiness. Many Christians through the centuries have found a daily examination to be a valuable spiritual practice. At the end of the day, they take a few minutes to review what happened during that day and how they responded to those events. This might lead into a prayer of contrition on the spot, and it also serves as a solid basis for celebrating the sacrament of penance periodically.

Called and Chosen; Called to Conversion

Martin Buber, in his little book *Ten Rungs: Hasidic Sayings*, shares this advice: "Everyone must have two pockets, so that he can reach into the one or the other, according to his needs. In his right pocket are to be the words: 'For my sake was the world created,' and in his left: 'I am but dust and ashes.'"[1]

---

[1] Martin Buber, *Ten Rungs: Hasidic Sayings* (New York: Schocken Books, 1947) 106.

In a similar way Christians should carry with them the two fundamental truths revealed in this period of the catechumenate. In one pocket, keep the words, "I am called and chosen." In the other pocket, keep this reminder: "I am called to conversion." Held together, these truths will keep us balanced. We will be sustained by the knowledge of God's love for us and constantly challenged by that love to deepen our conversion and commitment every day.

For Prayer

God is always faithful to those he calls; now it is your duty, as it is ours, both to be faithful to him in return and to strive courageously to reach the fullness of truth, which your election opens up before you (RCIA, no. 133).

Father of love and power, it is your will to establish everything in Christ and to draw us into his all-embracing love. Guide the elect of your Church: strengthen them in their vocation, build them into the kingdom of your Son, and seal them with the Spirit of your promise (RCIA, no. 135-B).

For Reflection and Discussion

1. Think of times that you have signed your name to some official document? What obligations did you incur as a result? What benefits?

2. Do you have a copy of your baptismal certificate? Do you think it would be a good idea to have it framed and displayed where you might see it often?

3. Do you think of yourself as chosen by God? For what did God choose you?

4. How do you enter into the season of Lent? What practices or prayers have you found helpful?

5. Have you experienced the celebration of the scrutinies on Lenten Sundays? If so, have the celebrations challenged and strengthened you along with the elect?

6. How often do you make use of the sacrament of penance? What role does it play in your spiritual growth and ongoing conversion?

8

Reborn to New Life

A new convert was being baptized in the river near the church.

The minister said to the candidate, "Now before I baptize you, I want to know if you believe in God the Father, the Son, and the Holy Spirit."

"Yes, I do," said the convert, and the minister pushed him under the water. He came up, sputtering and gasping.

The minister asked, "Do you believe all that our church believes?"

"Yes, I do," he replied, and the minister shoved him under a second time, holding him a bit longer than before. When he came up, he was choking and spitting out water.

"Now," said the minister, "I want you to tell this assembly in your own words what you believe."

The convert looked at him for a moment and replied, "I believe you're trying to drown me!"

For many Catholics, that form of baptism still seems foreign, yet current church documents show a preference for baptism by immersion rather than baptism by pouring. Pouring a small amount of water across someone's forehead suggests some kind of washing. Immersion three times under the water suggests (and feels like) drowning. This fuller form of baptism makes it easier to realize that baptism involves dying with Christ and rising with him to newness of life.

The liturgy that makes this clearest, of course, is the celebration of baptism during the Easter Vigil when we commemorate the paschal mystery most richly. Baptism is all about dying and rising with Christ. We come to new life only if we are willing to die with him.

Embracing Death

Language about dying and rising can be used so often that we begin to forget what radical language it is. Human beings, like all sentient creatures, do not generally welcome death. We fight it with every ounce of strength we can muster. We cling to life as long as we can. One witty psychiatrist notes that people say, "When I get to be ninety, I don't care if I live or die." And that, he says, is just how we feel until we reach eighty-nine! Then we want to live forever.

This resistance to death goes beyond mere physical death, too. We have a hard time accepting the death of a relationship or the death of a dream or the death of our plans. Every death, physical or spiritual, requires letting go, and we instinctively hold on tight.

Christ promises us everlasting life, but the road to eternal life leads through the cross. We must embrace death if we are to be reborn to new life. Jesus himself has shown us the way. By embracing the Father's will and accepting death, he was raised to new life. His resurrection stands as a promise to all who follow him into the paschal mystery.

Embracing death is another way to speak of conversion. Turning our lives over to the Lord requires a death to self. It involves letting go of many things that may have become so much a part of us that we think we cannot survive without them. We may need to die to habits of sin that have become ingrained. We may have to die to attitudes toward others that we have carried for years. We may need to put to death instinctive responses that are not in tune with the Gospel. We have to die to the selfishness and self-centeredness that seem to lie deep in the core of our beings.

> One Sunday morning the pastor noticed little Johnny staring up at the large plaque that hung in the vestibule of the church. The seven-year-old had been staring at the plaque for some time, so the pastor walked up, stood beside the boy, and said quietly, "Good morning, son."
>
> "Good morning, pastor" replied the youngster, focused on the plaque. "Sir, what is this?" Johnny asked.
>
> "Well, son, these are all the people who died in the service," replied the pastor.
>
> Soberly, they stood together, staring at the large plaque. Little Johnny's voice barely broke the silence when he asked quietly, "Which one, sir, the 8:30 or the 10:30?"

One might hope that lots of people die in every liturgical service we celebrate, since the liturgy constantly invites us to share Christ's death and resurrection. We are to die to sin that we might live Christ's life more fully. This is especially clear in baptism and the Eucharist, but it is reflected in all the other sacraments as well.

In varying degrees, all the sacraments express this theme. Baptism is our first immersion into Christ's dying and rising. The Eucharist is our central celebration of the death and resurrection of Christ. The sacrament of penance calls us to die to sin and renew our baptismal life. The anointing of the sick urges the patient to unite his or her sufferings with Christ, trusting in the promise of resurrection. Marriage and holy orders specify the vocations in which our dying and rising will occur.

So, too, the whole of Christian morality and spirituality can be understood as guidance in how to die to sin and rise to

fullness of life in Christ. Thus much of the Church's catechetical activity is aimed at teaching us how to die and rise.

Every time we face the need to embrace death, we need to
remind ourselves that we have already died with Christ and
have already begun to live a new life. Our Christian life is book-
ended by two major death-resurrection experiences: our baptism and our physical death. In between these two, the whole
of Christian life is marked by this leitmotif of dying and rising.

Accentuate the Positive

An unremitting focus on the need to die to self can be mis-
directed, however. The key to a healthy spiritual life is a proper
balance. There have been many periods in our history as a
Church when we have focused too exclusively on the negative
side of the conversion process. If the Church preaches only the
sinfulness of humanity and the threat of eternal damnation,
religion can easily become a matter of fear and self-hatred. That
is not the message Jesus proclaims in the Gospel.

The reason we should embrace death is not out of guilt or
self-loathing or fear. The only valid reason to embrace death is
to come to a fuller life. Jesus came, he said, that we "might
have life and have it more abundantly" (John 10:10). The challenge for us is to accept the gift of life that Jesus offers us.

The difficulty, of course, is that so many things that seem
to offer us abundant life really bring us death. Any sin we
choose, we really choose because it seems to offer us something good, something life-enhancing. It takes much wisdom
to judge what will truly bring us to the fullness of life. That
wisdom is available to us through the Scriptures and through
the tradition of the church community, but it is constantly
contradicted by the wisdom of the world around us. We must
choose what wisdom will guide our lives and keep choosing
again and again as we are confronted with new decisions and
new situations.

God's wisdom leads us to life. A good way to evaluate our progress on the road of conversion is whether we are becoming more fully alive. That is the purpose of living the paschal mystery. Just as Jesus could only arrive at the fullness of resurrected life by embracing the cross, so we come to fullness of life to the degree that we embrace death and allow God to raise us up.

A New Person, A New Life

The goal of all this dying and rising is expressed by St. Paul in various ways. He tells the Corinthians that "whoever is in Christ is a new creation" (2 Cor 5:17). He urges the Ephesians to "put on the new self, created in God's way in righteousness and holiness of truth" (Eph 4:24). He reminds the Romans that we were buried with Christ in baptism "so that, just as Christ was raised by the glory of the Father, we too might live in newness of life" (Rom 6:4). He goes even further in writing to the Galatians, saying "I live, no longer I, but Christ lives in me" (Gal 2:20).

All of these are ways of saying that we are called to live in a new way, a way that is different from those who have not been claimed by Christ and have not professed faith in him. The need for this difference in lifestyle becomes obvious when we compare the values of our current culture with the values of the Gospel. There was a time when those values were very similar, at least in theory. In recent times, however, the values of the culture have become increasingly different from the values of Jesus Christ.

This is a major challenge for the Church in our time, because we had become accustomed to assuming that the culture would support our values and reinforce appropriate behavior. It seems to be taking us a long time to come to grips with the fact that our current situation is quite similar to the conditions the Church faced in its earliest centuries. We are a minority within society, espousing values and a lifestyle that are very different from the culture and often facing rejection, if not outright persecution, as a result.

This is difficult for individual members of the Church as well. All of us have a desire to fit in, to belong, to be accepted. That makes it difficult to stand up for values that others reject or to live in a way that others ridicule. Here, too, we need to be willing to die to self and to our desire for acceptance if we are to be faithful to our baptismal commitment. The challenge is expressed in a question sometimes seen on bumper stickers: "If you were on trial for being a Christian, would there be enough evidence to convict you?"

Remembering that we have been baptized might lead us to examine our lives to see what values really motivate us. The values of the culture are constantly bombarding us from the media, from friends and coworkers, from politicians, and especially from advertising. It takes a constant vigilance to make sure that we are living by the values of Jesus Christ. If we cannot point to numerous issues on which our values differ from the values of contemporary culture, we may need to question our commitment to living out our baptism.

This is the reason that the Church calls us to renew our baptismal promises every Easter. After we have examined ourselves during Lent (in connection with the scrutinies of the catechumens), we are invited to formally commit ourselves once again to living out our baptism.

Too often, this annual baptismal renewal is glossed over and treated as inconsequential. It is intended to be much more than a token reminder of our baptism. If we take Lent seriously as a time to prepare for this moment, then the ritual renewal of vows should take on heightened importance in our lives.

As more and more dioceses move confirmation back into its traditional place before First Communion, some worry about how we will get teenagers to renew their baptismal commitment if confirmation is no longer celebrated after puberty.

The broader answer is that we need a vibrant youth ministry in every parish, but this Easter renewal of vows could also be a significant moment for teens if it has become so for the whole parish.

In a similar vein, many Catholics make it a practice to begin each day with such a recommitment. This "morning offering" can be an effective way to remind ourselves on a daily basis of our identity as the baptized. We might even say such a prayer as we shower or wash in the morning, remembering the water of the font that gave us new life. We begin each day with the experience of water. It is good to begin each day as though we just stepped out of the font.

For Prayer

Father, you give us grace through sacramental signs, which tell us of the wonders of your unseen power. In baptism we use your gift of water, which you have made a rich symbol of the grace you give us in this sacrament. At the very dawn of creation your Spirit breathed on the waters, making them the wellspring of all holiness. The waters of the great flood you made a sign of the waters of baptism that make an end of sin and a new beginning of goodness. Through the waters of the Red Sea you led Israel out of slavery to be an image of God's holy people, set free from sin by baptism. In the waters of the Jordan your Son was baptized by John and anointed with the Spirit. Your Son willed that water and blood should flow from his side as he hung upon the cross. After his resurrection he told his disciples: "Go out and teach all nations, baptizing them in the name of the Father, and of the Son, and of the Holy Spirit." Father, look now with love upon your Church and unseal for her the fountain of baptism. By the power of the Holy spirit give to this water the grace of your Son, so that in the sacrament of baptism all those whom you have created in your likeness may be cleansed from sin and rise to a new birth of innocence by water and the Holy Spirit. We ask you, Father, with your Son to send the Holy Spirit upon the waters of this font. May all who are buried with Christ in the death of baptism rise also with him to newness of life (RCIA, no. 222).

For Reflection and Discussion

1. Have you ever seen baptism by immersion? If so, what did the experience say to you about the meaning of baptism? If not, what do you think the experience might communicate to you?

2. Can you name times in your life when you had to embrace some form of death? Can you see how new life came after that embrace?

3. Have you taken part in the Easter Vigil? Was it a good experience for you? Would you encourage others to take part? What would you say to them?

4. In what areas do you see our culture's values in conflict with the values of the Gospel? How have you struggled with this conflict in your own life?

5. If you were on trial for being a Christian, what evidence might others offer to prove that you are?

6. How significant to you is the renewal of baptismal promises at Easter? How do you think it could be made more meaningful?

9

Living in the Spirit

Jerry was walking across the road when he was struck by a car. He landed on his head, which caused him to be comatose for two days before he finally regained consciousness. When he opened his eyes, his wife, Jodi, was there beside him.

Jerry held Jodi's hands and said meaningfully: "You have always been by my side. When I was a struggling university student, I failed again and again. You were there beside me, encouraging me to go on trying."

Jodi squeezed his hands as he continued: "When I went for all the major interviews and failed to clinch any of the jobs, you were there beside me, cutting out more ads for me to pursue." He continued: "Then I started to work at this little firm and finally got to handle a big contract. I blew it because of one little mistake. And you were there beside me. Then I finally got another job after being laid off for some time. But I never seemed to be promoted, and my hard work was not recognized. I remained in the same position from the day I joined the company until now, and you were still beside me."

Jodi's eyes brimmed with tears as she listened to Jerry. "And now", he said, "I have met with an accident and when I wake up, you are here beside me. There's something I'd really like to say to you."

> Jodi flung herself on the bed to hug Jerry, sobbing with emotion. Then he said, "I think you bring me bad luck!"

Though Jerry concluded his companion was a curse, having someone at our side through thick and thin is usually seen as a blessing. The Christian tradition speaks of a divine companion who is always with us, the Holy Spirit. Many members of the Church, though, seem largely unaware of this advocate who stays with us no matter what life brings our way. The Spirit is not only invisible but often unnoticed as well.

This seems to be more common in the Western Church than in the Eastern. Christians of the Eastern rites have paid more attention to the Holy Spirit throughout history and have a more highly developed devotion to the Holy Spirit. Many Christians in the West seldom address prayer to the Holy Spirit and seldom rely upon the Spirit for guidance and strength.

The Meaning of Confirmation

In the West, attention to the Spirit reaches its high point around the celebration of the sacrament of confirmation. Unfortunately, this is a sacrament that suffers from much confusion and misunderstanding in our time.

The Second Vatican Council (1962–65) called for the rite of confirmation to be revised and for "the intimate connection which this sacrament has with the whole of Christian initiation . . . to be more clearly set forth" (Constitution on the Sacred Liturgy, no. 71).[1] This intimate connection is expressed clearly in the Rite of Christian Initiation of Adults:

> In accord with the ancient practice followed in the Roman liturgy, adults are not to be baptized without receiving

[1] *The Constitution on the Sacred Liturgy of the Second Vatican Council and the Motu Proprio of Pope Paul VI with a Commentary by Gerard S. Sloyan* (Glen Rock, N.J.: Paulist Press, 1964) 54.

confirmation immediately afterward, unless some seri-
ous reason stands in the way. The conjunction of the two
celebrations signifies the unity of the paschal mystery,
the close link between the mission of the Son and the
outpouring of the Holy Spirit, and the connection between the two sacraments through which the Son and
the Holy Spirit come with the Father to those who are
baptized (no. 215).

The intimate connection among the three sacraments of
initiation is much less obvious in our current practice with
those baptized as infants. The universal law of the Church lists
the age of discretion as the proper age for confirmation, with
the implication that confirmation is thus celebrated before
First Eucharist. However, the law also allows the bishops of a
country to choose another age for pastoral reasons. In the
United States, after much discussion and long delay, the bishops could only agree to set the age at a range between seven
and eighteen. As a result, some dioceses confirm before First
Communion, others confirm at junior high age, and still others
defer confirmation until sometime in high school. In the latter
two patterns, the traditional order of the sacraments of initiation is changed.

One result of such separation of these three sacraments of
initiation is that many people have tried to understand and explain the meaning of confirmation without much reference to
baptism and the Eucharist. This has led to some interesting
but ultimately confusing ideas, such as the notion that confirmation is some kind of sacrament of maturity, akin to puberty
rites in tribal societies. The fallacy of this view is evident when
we recall that the Church has confirmed infants at their baptism for 2000 years in the East and for much of that time in
the West.

If confirmation is not about maturity, what does it mean?
We can get a healthy perspective when we consider the inte-

gral celebration of the three sacraments of initiation at the Easter Vigil. Those who are baptized are confirmed in the same ceremony. Their baptism expresses their incorporation into the death and resurrection of Christ, which is most evident when baptism is celebrated with full immersion. The anointing with oil after the water bath of baptism expresses the gift of the Holy Spirit and the consecration of the baptized as members of Christ, who is priest, prophet, and king.

In this integral celebration it is not possible to separate the effects of these two ritual moments from each other. We can only rise to new life in Christ through the power of the Spirit. We are given the Spirit by our incorporation into Christ; thus infants who are only baptized already receive the Holy Spirit. We share in Christ's roles of priest, prophet, and king because we are incorporated into him through baptism, yet it is the anointing that has been seen for centuries as the symbol of conferring the Spirit's power that enables us to fulfill these roles.

Confirmation and baptism are so closely interrelated that they might be described as two sides of the same coin. Each ritual moment (water bath and anointing) emphasizes a different aspect of initiation, but each depends on the other. This is why Vatican II called for stressing the connection between these two sacraments.

Anointed in the Spirit

The different emphasis expressed by these two ritual moments focuses our attention on the gift of the Spirit when we are anointed in confirmation. Those who are incorporated into the Body of Christ are gifted with the abiding presence of the Holy Spirit. It is this indwelling of the Spirit that makes us temples of the Trinity, for the Spirit is never separated from the Father and the Son. Any closeness we have with God is a result of the Spirit's presence. It is certainly appropriate, then, to call our relationship to God our "spiritual" life.

The foundation of the spiritual life is responding to the promptings of the Holy Spirit within us. Our growth in holiness can be measured by how attentive we become to the voice of the Spirit and how willing we are to listen to that voice.

Listening is often a difficult thing to do. We are usually much better at talking to God than listening. Moreover, the pace of contemporary life makes it a challenge for many of us to find any time for silence and listening in our daily routine. Taking such time regularly, however, is essential if we really want to grow in our relationship with the Lord.

The first step, of course, is simply to carve out a time and a place where we can slow down and sit in silence with God. Here's how Bishop Joseph McKinney, in a talk to young people, once described the process of listening to the Spirit:

> At the end of every day, I find a quiet place. If there is a quiet corner, I sit down in my "Holy Spirit Chair." If it is too noisy, I take a walk or a ride. Then I try to get everything out of my mind. I concentrate by trying to look deep inside myself . . .way down deep . . . because Jesus tells us that the Holy Spirit is within us. I find him very deep in my heart or as some people say today, at gut level. Then I wait to see what happens. The Holy Spirit doesn't use words, but slowly something that happened during the day starts coming up. Now I start to see it differently. Sometimes it is a wonderful opportunity that I missed. Sometimes it is like a seed. Someone said something or something important happened, or perhaps I just saw someone and they left an impression on me. As I continue to look at it—no words now because this is listening time—a new conviction starts to grow inside of me. That is the Holy Spirit speaking.

If we listen for that voice and then act on the new conviction that the Spirit fosters, then our lives will be shaped by divine guidance. That's certainly part of what it means to live as people who have been "born of water and Spirit" (John 3:5).

The Holy Spirit is often described in the tradition as the Spirit of Love, and theologians even describe the Holy Spirit as the bond of love between the Father and the Son. It is the power of the Holy Spirit dwelling within us that enables us to love as God loves. Because it is the bond of love in Christ that unites us as one body in the Church, the Holy Spirit is also called the Spirit of Unity. We recall this fact constantly in prayer and in the liturgy when we conclude prayers with the phrase "in the unity of the Holy Spirit."

If the Holy Spirit is a spirit of love and unity, then those who live by the Spirit will be people who strive to love as God loves and to build up the unity of the community of believers. Those who live under the guidance of the Spirit will not be lone rangers who think they can live as Christians without needing others. Spirit-filled people are community minded people who recognize their intimate bonds with every other member of the Body of Christ.

The Spirit who prompts us to love one another in the Church also prompts us to reach beyond the Church to share the love of God and the good news of Jesus Christ to others. The events of the first Pentecost express clearly the Spirit's role in energizing the frightened disciples to preach the Gospel. The Spirit can energize us in a similar way today if we are open to the Spirit's power. This is why confirmation has often been linked to the call to mission that is inherent in baptism.

Those who live their baptism daily are vitally aware of the presence of the Spirit and attentive to the Spirit's promptings. They are people who love with a kind of love that only God's presence within them makes possible. They are people committed to sharing faith within the church community and sharing the good news with those who do not yet know Christ.

For Prayer

All-powerful God, Father of our Lord Jesus Christ, by water and the Holy Spirit you freed your sons and daughters from sin and gave them new life. Send your Holy Spirit upon them to be their helper and guide. Give them the spirit of wisdom and understanding, the spirit of right judgment and courage, the spirit of knowledge and reverence. Fill them with the spirit of wonder and awe in your presence (RCIA, no. 234).

For Reflection and Discussion

1. How often do you pray to the Holy Spirit? How often do you listen for the Spirit's voice? In what ways has the Spirit guided your life?

2. How would you explain the meaning of confirmation? What is the purpose of this sacrament?

3. What role does the Holy Spirit play in the life of your parish? If awareness of the Spirit needs to be heightened, how might that be accomplished?

4. How would you explain to someone why the Catholic Church currently confirms infants, child catechumens, and adult catechumens right after baptism but delays confirmation for those baptized as infants in the West?

5. At what age do you think confirmation should be celebrated? Can you give reasons for your position?

10

Gathered Around the Table

A preacher was completing a temperance sermon. With great expression he said, "If I had all the beer in the world, I'd take it and throw it into the river." With even greater emphasis he said, "And if I had all the wine in the world, I'd take it and throw it into the river." And in conclusion, he said, "And if I had all the whiskey in the world, I'd take it and throw it into the river." He sat down.

The song leader then stood very cautiously and announced with a smile, "For our closing song, let us sing hymn number 365: 'Shall We Gather at the River.'"

Those who are filled with the Holy Spirit, in contrast to those who might yearn for liquid spirits, gather not at the river but around the table of the Lord. The celebration of the Eucharist is the third and climactic sacrament of initiation. After going into the watery tomb with Christ and rising to new life, after being anointed in the Holy Spirit, new members of the Church share with the community for the first time in the eucharistic meal that defines the community.

This third sacrament of initiation is different from the first two because it is repeatable. We can only be baptized and confirmed once in a lifetime, but we are invited to share at the table of the Lord hundreds and thousands of times. Baptism and confirmation stand as the doorway into the ongoing life of the Church, and the Eucharist marks the community's life and identity.

One Body in Christ

We who are baptized are incorporated into the Body of Christ. This fundamental truth can provide countless hours of fruitful meditation and contemplation. Our identity as members of the Church is defined around the table. We who share the body and blood of Christ *are* the Body of Christ. We are so intimately united with all other members of the faith community that our tradition, starting with St. Paul, can find no better image than the unity of the human body. As one part of the body depends on all the rest, so each of us is dependent on the rest of the body for our spiritual health.

The Catholic tradition is very clear that the celebration of the Eucharist transforms the bread and wine into the very body and blood of Christ. This is a great mystery and a core belief of our faith community. We do not merely share a memory of Christ and some vague sense of his presence. We share in his body and blood, present in a way that enables us to touch and taste and know him to be with us intimately and fully.

Sometimes, however, this basic tenet of faith has led some of us to overlook other fundamental truths about the Eucharist. Focusing too exclusively on the fact of Christ's presence can lead us to forget the purpose of his presence. As St. Thomas Aquinas taught in the thirteenth century, the purpose of the Eucharist is the unity of the Christian community. Christ feeds us with his body and blood so that we will become ever more fully his body. The purpose of the Eucharist is not to transform bread and wine (though it does that) but to transform us.

This link between the sacramental Body of Christ and the mystical Body of Christ (the Church) lies at the core of the mystery of the Eucharist. To properly celebrate this sacrament, we must recognize the connection between the two. St. Paul indicated as much early in the Church's life: "For anyone who eats and drinks without discerning the body, eats and drinks a judgment on himself" (1 Cor 11:29).

Thus, when we share the body and blood of the Lord, we must always remember that we share it with all the other members of his body. Communion is never a private matter between Jesus and me. It always unites me to all those who share the one bread and one cup.

The challenge of the Eucharist, then, is to embrace our own identity as part of the Body of Christ and to embrace all the other members of the body. When we say "Amen" as we receive the body and the blood of Christ, we are signaling our willingness to be the Body of Christ in union with all the other members of that body.

The Call to Sacrifice

Being the Body of Christ in the world requires us to imitate Christ, and that may bring us what it brought him. The Eucharist reminds us of this risk every time we celebrate it, for every Eucharistic prayer proclaims his death and resurrection and invites us to share in his sacrifice.

The liturgy itself requires a certain amount of sacrifice from each of us. To share in one common act of worship, we all must surrender our personal tastes and desires. We can't have the liturgy just the way we'd like it. Moreover, we have to open our hearts and our hands to those around us; we cannot stay safely isolated from the demands other people make on us. Even taking an active part in the singing and responses requires that we make an effort and, at least at times, go beyond our comfort zone.

These small sacrifices that are required in order to enter into the act of worship point us toward the larger sacrifices that may be required of us in daily life if we are truly to live out our baptismal commitment. Following Christ means that we must be vulnerable—both because we are called to speak the truth that often brings persecution and because we are called to reach out in love to all people. This flies in the face of our natural instinct for self-preservation and self-protection, but it is an essential part of living out our baptismal mission.

Saying "Amen"

Our willingness to share in Christ's sacrifice is expressed by a simple but powerful word. The Hebrew word "Amen" is often translated as "So be it," which is an accurate translation. The significance of our "Amen," however, becomes more apparent when we trace the Hebrew word back to its original root. It comes from a verb in ancient Hebrew that means "to pound in one's tent stake." This comes from a time when the Hebrew people were nomads in the desert. Without a tent to shield you from the heat of the noonday sun and to protect you from the cold of the desert night, you do not survive long in the desert. Thus "Amen" suggests something like our English expression, "I'd stake my life on it."

When we sing "Amen" at the end of the Eucharistic prayer, we stake our lives on following the example of Jesus, whose faithfulness to the Father led him to death on the cross. When we say "Amen" as we receive the body and the blood of the Lord, we stake our lives on being part of the body of Christ and signal our willingness to have our bodies broken and our blood poured out for the sake of our brothers and sisters as Jesus did.

"Amen" is a short word that has deep implications. We might meditate many hours on the meaning of what we say with those few letters. If we do, we may come to say "Amen" only with fear and trembling, for it sums up the meaning of our lives.

Disciples Around the Table

Sustaining our commitment and our strength for being Christ's presence in the world is the reason the church community has always seen regular participation in the Sunday Eucharist as essential. As we go about our lives and our work throughout the week, we function as the Body of Christ dispersed throughout the world. When we gather on Sunday, we reassemble as the visible body of the Lord. We are nourished from the table of the word and the table of the bread and wine, so that we will have the strength to go out again to carry on the work of Christ for another week.

Through baptism we have been added to the company of disciples who gather around the table of the Lord. Disciples are those who learn from the Lord and imitate him. We who are disciples are also sent as apostles, dismissed from the eucharistic table to carry on the mission of Christ to the world.

This is why the catechumenate comes to its climax not at the font but around the table. We are not given new life in baptism for our sake alone. We are called to the font in order to join the company of those charged by Christ to carry on his work. We come repeatedly to the table to be nourished and strengthened so that we will be able to fulfill this sacred charge.

Every week when we gather for the eucharistic meal, we renew the meaning of our baptism. As we were incorporated into the death and resurrection of Christ in the waters of the font, so we remember his dying and his rising in every Eucharist. As we became part of the Body of Christ in baptism, we renew our identity as part of the body every time we share the body and the blood of the Lord. As we were commissioned to carry on the work of Christ at our baptism (and confirmation), we are sent forth from every Eucharist to continue that mission.

An Attitude of Gratitude

What draws us to the table, though, is not a weighty sense of responsibility but a joyful sense of gratitude. The Eucharist is fundamentally a prayer of thanksgiving, as its very name suggests (*eucharistia* is Greek for thanksgiving). We gather because we have been so richly blessed. We gather to recall again all that God has done for us throughout history and throughout our own lives. We gather to thank and praise God for the many gifts we have received, not the least of which is the gift of the Eucharist itself. We gather to thank God for calling us to share the divine life and for entrusting to us the work of preparing the way for God's kingdom.

If the Eucharist defines our identity, then we should be people who live in a state of constant thanksgiving. At the beginning of every Eucharistic prayer we say: "It is right to give him thanks and praise." Eucharistic Prayer II continues: "Father, it is our duty and our salvation, always and everywhere, to give you thanks through your beloved Son, Jesus Christ." Always and everywhere we are called to give God thanks, because always and everywhere we are blessed by God.

It is easy, in daily living, to forget how blessed we are. It seems natural to focus on the things that go wrong, the things we don't have, the things we wish were different. Weekly celebration of the Eucharist should constantly remind us of the multitude of reasons we have to be grateful.

It is also helpful to remind ourselves more often than once a week. Every day, many times a day, we might stop briefly to "count our blessings" in a spirit of gratitude. A quick prayer of thanksgiving to God could be offered dozens of times each day if we are aware that everything we have and use is a gift from God. Every bite we eat, the water we use to drink and to cleanse, the energy that gives us light and heat and cooling, the clothes we wear, the books we read, the media we use for news and entertainment, the nature that surrounds us, even the breath that keeps us alive—all is gift, and all should prompt us to give thanks.

It is gratitude that ultimately leads to our good works and our efforts to bring about the kingdom. We do not do good works in order to earn God's favor. We do them because we have already been blessed by God. Whatever good we can claim in our lives is really a response to God's gracious goodness toward us. Our whole lives thus become an act of gratitude, and we can rightfully be called eucharistic people.

Those who live their baptism every day live in gratitude, gather regularly around the table of the Lord, and go forth from that meal to spread the good news of God's love and generous grace to all people. They are truly eucharistic people.

For Prayer

Look with favor on the offering of your Church in which we show forth the paschal sacrifice of Christ entrusted to us. Through the power of your Spirit of love include us now and for ever among the members of your Son, whose body and blood we share. Almighty Father, by our sharing in this mystery enliven us with your Spirit and conform us to the image of your Son. Strengthen the bonds of our communion with N. our pope, and N. our bishop, with all bishops, priests, and deacons, and all your holy people. Keep your Church alert in faith to the signs of the times and eager to accept the challenge of the gospel. Open our hearts to the needs of all humanity, so that sharing their grief and anguish, their joy and hope, we may faithfully bring them the good news of salvation and advance together on the way to your kingdom (Eucharistic Prayer for Various Needs and Occasions, III).

For Reflection and Discussion

1. What does the Mass mean to you? How important is it in your life?

2. How would you explain the meaning of Communion to a non-Christian? How would you explain it to another Christian?

3. Did you find anything in this chapter that challenged your thinking about the Eucharist? If so, why was it challenging?

4. How do you share in Christ's sacrifice? What implications does the celebration of the Mass have for your daily life?

5. How often do you thank God for the gifts that fill your life? If you need to deepen your sense of gratitude, how might you do so?

11

What Have I Done?

A young couple got married and left on their honeymoon. When they got back, the bride immediately called her mother.

Her mother asked, "How was the honeymoon?"

"Oh, mama," she replied, "the honeymoon was wonderful! So romantic." Then suddenly she burst out crying. "But, mama, as soon as we returned Sam started using the most horrible language—things I'd never heard before! I mean, all these awful four-letter words! You've got to come get me and take me home. Please, mama!"

"Sarah, Sarah," her mother said, "calm down! Tell me, what could be so awful? What four-letter words?"

"Please don't make me tell you, mama," wept the daughter, "I'm so embarrassed; they're just too awful! Come get me, please!"

"Darling, baby, you must tell me what has you so upset. Tell your mother these horrible four-letter words!"

Still sobbing, the bride said, "Oh, mama, words like DUST, WASH, IRON, COOK . . . !"

Most newlyweds, men as well as women, come to a point at which they ask themselves, "What have I done? What have I gotten myself into?" I heard one woman on the radio admit that it hit her as she was walking down the aisle at the end of the wedding! The Church wisely recognizes that similar doubts may afflict those who have come through the catechumenate and celebrated the sacraments of initiation. Thus the Rite of Christian Initiation of Adults prescribes a fourth period that occurs after the celebration of the Easter sacraments. This is called the period of mystagogy, a word that clearly needs some explanation.

Understanding from Experience

The term comes from the Greek *mystagogia*, meaning the study of the mysteries. The early Church used the term "mysteries" to refer to what we call the sacraments. The primary purpose of this period of mystagogy, therefore, is to probe more deeply the meaning of the sacraments, especially those that were celebrated at the Easter Vigil, the sacraments of initiation. The formal period of mystagogy for the newly baptized extends through the fifty days from Easter Sunday until Pentecost. The U.S. bishops also require an extended mystagogy lasting for a full year beyond this initial period.

The foundation of mystagogy is a basic principle of education: We can best understand something after we have experienced it. While we can learn much about God or a sacrament in theory before an experience, there are dimensions of reality that can only be grasped after the experience. We correctly say to someone who has lost a spouse, for example, that we cannot really understand what they are feeling, though we may try to empathize with them. One who has lost his or her own spouse, however, can understand much more.

The Church through the centuries has learned that there are dimensions of the sacramental experience that cannot be grasped in theory alone. Reflection after the experience of the sacraments of initiation offers a richness and depth that cannot be attained beforehand.

Ongoing Mystagogy

Of course, the full meaning of any of the sacraments may not be grasped in the period of mystagogy, either. That's the reason the bishops call for extended mystagogy. We might even say that all of Christian life after baptism is a process of ongoing mystagogy. It may take us the rest of our lives to fully grasp the significance of what happened to us when we died and rose with Christ. In fact, it may not be until we die and rise the final time as we move from this life into the next that we will fully comprehend what it means to share Christ's death and resurrection.

Another indication of this ongoing nature of mystagogy is that the Rite of Christian Initiation of Adults calls for the mystagogical catechesis of the newly baptized to take place at the homily of the Sunday Masses of the Easter season. These homilies are addressed not only to the newly baptized but to the whole assembly. Every year we return to our roots and reflect together on what it means to have been initiated into the mystery of Christ. As the RCIA puts it, "This is a time for the community and the neophytes together to grow in deepening their grasp of the paschal mystery and in making it a part of their lives through meditation on the Gospel, sharing in the Eucharist, and doing the works of charity" (no. 244).

The ongoing character of mystagogy can remind us that our formation as Christians is never really finished. We are on a life-long journey, and the Holy Spirit keeps calling us deeper into the mystery of the Trinity. There is a natural temptation we all face to begin to see ourselves as a finished product, to think that we have finished learning about our faith once we graduate from high school or college or to see ourselves as fully formed Christians when we reach some threshold of our life. The Church's yearly return to mystagogy every Easter reminds us that we all have more growing to do.

Journey into Mystery

The reason that we can never finish deepening our understanding of the sacraments is that they draw us into the realm of mystery. A mystery is not something that is totally unknowable, but every true mystery exceeds our capacity to grasp it completely. There is always more that we can explore, more insights that are available, more depth to probe. Mystery is bigger than the human mind, so it eludes our control.

Encountering mystery is the purpose of the sacraments. While the sacraments have many other effects that we can name, their central purpose is to facilitate an encounter with the divine. Ultimately this is the purpose of everything the Church does. It is this encounter with mystery that provides the energy and strength to carry on the Church's mission. If contact with mystery is missing, religion can easily become a social gathering or a mere social service agency.

Remembering that we are dealing with mystery is crucial to a proper understanding of the Christian life. Following Christ is not ultimately a matter of rules and doctrines. Those exist in order to guide us into the mystery. The difficulty is that dealing with mystery is risky. One cannot predict the outcome when a person truly encounters the divine. It is often difficult, even for the person involved, to describe the encounter or to define its consequences.

This unpredictability often prompts us to avoid the encounter. We instinctively prefer the safe and secure world of rules and dogma, where we can feel in control. Annie Dillard, a contemporary mystical writer, puts the issue well in her book *Teaching a Stone to Talk:*

> On the whole, I do not find Christians, outside of the catacombs, sufficiently sensible of conditions. Does anyone have the foggiest idea what sort of power we so blithely invoke? Or, as I suspect, does no one believe a word of it? The churches are children playing on the

floor with their chemistry sets, making up a batch of TNT to kill a Sunday morning. It is madness to wear ladies' hats and straw hats and velvet hats to church; we should all be wearing crash helmets. Ushers should issue life preservers and signal flares; they should lash us to our pews. For the sleeping god may wake someday and take offense, or the waking god may draw us out to where we can never return.[1]

We need to approach the liturgy with more humility. We are not in control of what will happen during worship. We can prepare the way for an encounter with God, but we cannot make it happen. And we have no way to predict in advance what will happen to us if we do meet the Lord. We must give up our illusion of being in charge and let God be God.

To have any hope of a true encounter with the divine mystery, we also have to approach with expectation. Sometimes we miss the Lord because we do not really allow for the possibility that God might touch us and change our lives. Of course, sometimes we avoid such an encounter precisely because it might call for such change. Rudolf Otto, in his classic work *The Idea of the Holy*,[2] defined the holy as the *mysterium tremendum et fascinans*. The mystery fascinates us and draws us in, but it also terrifies us and scares us away. We have to allow the fascination to overcome our fears.

Living with Mystery

Most of us would benefit from a deeper awareness of mystery beyond the liturgy, too. It is so easy to live our lives on the

---

[1] Annie Dillard, *Teaching a Stone to Talk* (New York: Harper Colophon, 1982) 41–42.

[2] Rudolf Otto, *The Idea of the Holy*, John W. Harvey, trans. (Oxford: Oxford University Press, 1923; 2nd ed., 1950 [Das Heilige, 1917]).

surface without paying attention to the deeper reality that undergirds all things. Much of spiritual growth is about learning how to see more deeply into all reality.

Although the term mystagogy is applied to the final period of the catechumenal journey, that period does not stand alone. The newly baptized do not suddenly develop an openness to mystery at the moment of their baptism. Mystagogical awareness must be fostered throughout their formation.

The RCIA really calls the Church to a more intensive focus on mystery. This is reflected in the insistence of the *General Directory for Catechesis* that all catechesis in the Church is to be modeled on catechesis in the catechumenate. This method of catechesis, sometimes called liturgical catechesis, is really mystagogical. It seeks to prepare people for the liturgical experience and then to reflect on the experience afterwards. The experience, the encounter with God, is central to this kind of catechesis. The goal of catechesis is not just to teach about God but to lead people to the experience of God and then to help them to articulate what happened to them when they met the Lord.

Those who have encountered the Lord in baptism and in the Eucharist are called, therefore, to live with a constant awareness of the mystery that surrounds us. Through their experience of God mediated through material elements of water and oil and bread and wine and through the human beings who reveal God's face to them, they have learned to look beneath the surface of reality. They know that there is always more than meets the eye.

Contemplating the Mystery

The baptized are thus called to a life of contemplation. Contemplation is not reserved for monks and hermits. It is a way of responding to life that refuses to live only on the surface of things. It is a way of seeing all of reality, recognizing that anyone or anything we encounter can become translucent or even transparent, revealing the mystery hidden within.

Such contemplative living leads us to a respect and care for all of creation. If every part of God's creation can be a means to encounter the Lord, then everything around us deserves our care. What sense does it make to use water as the instrument of divine life in baptism and then pollute the streams from which our water comes? How can we use bread and wine as the means of Christ's bodily presence in the Eucharist and not be concerned about the depletion of the soil that produces these gifts?

Even more critically, perhaps, how can we see the face of Christ in our brothers and sisters in church and not recognize him when we meet other human beings on the street? Awareness of the mystery at the heart of all creation should certainly heighten our awareness of the mystery of God's presence in all those who were created in the divine image and likeness.

Those who live their baptism daily live in continual awareness of the mystery of God's presence that permeates our world. They look for the Lord in the liturgy and are also alert to the divine presence at any time and in any place. They allow God to touch them and to change them often, and the energy from these encounters gives them strength to follow the Lord faithfully and enthusiastically.

For Prayer

God, the all-powerful Father of our Lord Jesus Christ, has given us a new birth by water and the Holy Spirit and forgiven all our sins. May he also keep us faithful to our Lord Jesus Christ for ever and ever (RCIA, no. 240).

Father, you give your Church constant growth by adding new members to your family. Help us to put into action in our lives the baptism we have received with faith. We ask this through our Lord, Jesus Christ, your Son, who lives and reigns with you and the Holy Spirit, one God, for ever and ever (*Sacramentary*, Easter Monday).

For Reflection and Discussion

1. If another parishioner asked you what "mystagogy" means, how would you answer?

2. How has your own understanding of and appreciation for the sacraments changed over the years?

3. Does the preaching during the Easter season in your parish help you to reflect on what it means to be baptized and confirmed and sharing in the Eucharist? Do you focus your own prayer and reflection on Scripture around those themes during the Fifty Days of Easter?

4. Why do you think people in our culture find it difficult to deal with mystery? How often does your prayer lead you into an awareness of the mystery of God that surrounds you?

5. Do you think of yourself as a contemplative person? What practices could you adopt that would make you more aware of the mystery that lies at the heart of all things?

12

Looking Back, Looking Forward

The comedian Jerry Lewis used to say that the best wedding present he received was a film of the ceremony (this was in the pre-VCR era). When things got rough in the marriage, he would go into the den, close the door, put the film in the projector, run it through backwards, and walk away a free man!

It would be helpful for Christians to have films of their baptisms, too—not to play them backwards, but to view them periodically to remind themselves of the meaning of their lives. Most Catholics were baptized as infants, so they have no personal memories of their own baptisms. Only a few, I suspect, have videos or films of the event to watch now. That's one reason that the Church celebrates the baptismal journey of catechumens (and often infant baptisms as well) in the midst of the parish community. It gives all of us a chance to recall and reclaim our own baptismal identity.

Those who have entered the Church through the catechumenate have their own memories to recall. It can be a very healthy thing for them to return periodically to those memories to renew their enthusiasm and to deepen their commitment. Like married couples reviewing their wedding albums, the baptized can recall the significant moments of their conversion journey and reclaim their identity as members of the Body of Christ.

Those without such personal memories or video reminders might best recall the meaning of their baptisms by sharing in the baptismal journey of catechumens and by rejoicing together with parents who bring their children to be baptized in the midst of the parish community. Just as joining in the celebration of someone else's wedding offers an opportunity for all married couples to renew their own commitment, so sharing in another's baptism calls all the baptized to deeper awareness and dedication.

The Order of the Faithful

At whatever age we were baptized, we entered the most basic order in the Church, the order of the faithful. Catechumens move from the order of catechumens into the order of the faithful when they celebrate the Easter sacraments. Within the Church, there are other specialized orders of ministry (bishop, priest, deacon), but the largest and most fundamental order is the order of the faithful. The other orders exist for the sake of the faithful. As St. Augustine said of his role as bishop: "Though I am terrified by what I am for you, I am comforted by what I am with you. For you I am a bishop, but with you I am a Christian. The first is the name of an office I have accepted, the second is a grace. The first involves danger, the second salvation" (Sermon 340, 1).

Too often in the past we have overemphasized the role and dignity of the ministerial orders to the detriment of the order of the faithful. It can seem at times as though the order of the faithful exists to serve the bishops, priests and deacons, but it should be the opposite. In truth, we are all to serve one another in the Lord, and the difference in the various orders is not a matter of higher or lower dignity or importance. In Christ, all are equally unimportant and all are equally important.

What is crucial is that the baptized reclaim the dignity of their order. The order of the faithful is the order to which the mission of the Church has been entrusted by the Lord. It is the task of the bishop, priest, and deacon to help the laity carry out that mission, but these special orders do not replace the faithful. They may have the burden of authority to administer the Church and to coordinate the various ministries of the faithful, but the mission belongs to the whole Church.

Embracing the Mission

That's the other side of the coin of the dignity of the order of the faithful. The faithful are important in God's eyes because they have been called to carry on the work of Christ in the world today. It's an example of the ancient motto *noblesse oblige*. The nobility of the baptized carries with it the obligation to live up to the trust God has placed in us.

As we have noted earlier, baptism is not primarily a gift given to us for our personal salvation. God could save us, as God saves many people, in other ways. We who have been called to baptism are called to carry on the mission of the Church. We are to be the Body of Christ in the world today, making his presence real to those around us and making his love felt by those who need us.

It is baptism, not holy orders, that constitutes the Church as church. Through baptism we have been called by God to be the Body of Christ in the world today. We exist as Church, we form the Body of Christ, in order to continue his work. The call to mission is fundamental to the identity of the Church and thus fundamental to the meaning of baptism.

> A hurricane blew across the Caribbean. It didn't take long for the expensive yacht to be swamped by high waves, sinking without a trace. There were only two survivors: the boat's owner, Dr. Jonas, and its steward, George, who managed to swim to the closest island. After reaching the

deserted strip of land, the steward was crying and very upset that they would never be found. The other man was quite calm, relaxing against a tree.

"Dr. Jonas, Dr. Jonas, how can you be so calm?" cried George. "We're going to die on this lonely island. We'll never be discovered here."

"Sit down and listen to what I have to say, George," began the confident Dr. Jonas. "Five years ago I gave the United Way $500,000 and gave another $500,000 to the United Jewish Appeal. I donated the same amounts four years ago and, three years ago, since I did very well in the stock market, I contributed $750,000 to each. Last year business was good, so the two charities each got a million dollars."

"So what?" shouted George.

"Well, it's time for their annual fund drives, and I know they're going to find me," smiled Dr. Jonas.

I've heard many Christians express similar sentiments about the Church. "All they want is my money," some say. For centuries, most lay Catholics assumed that the work of the Church was the sole, or at least the primary, responsibility of the ordained clergy and the vowed religious. They were seen as "the Church"; they were the real Christians. The laity were supposed to obey church leaders and to support them by prayer and financial contributions, but the work of the Church was up to the "professionals."

One can blame this view on the clergy who claimed power and authority in the Church and thus disenfranchised the laity, and there is surely some truth to that explanation. But I suspect there is another dimension that led to this view of the Church. There is a natural temptation, of course, to shrink from this call of God. It is always easier to focus the responsibility on someone else. If the clergy and religious wanted to claim the work of the Church, there were certainly many lay Christians who were happy to let them take it!

The renewal of Christian initiation calls us back to a view of the Church based on baptism, in which the responsibility for the life and work of the Church is shared by all the baptized, whether ordained, religious, or lay.

The challenge for each of us is the same: to accept the responsibility, to embrace the mission. The more we identify with Christ in our lives, the more obvious it becomes that we are called to make him present wherever we go. Christ wants to touch and heal our world through us. In our families, in our workplaces, in our neighborhoods, in our organizations, Christ wants to work through us. It is a great responsibility, for we have the power to open the way of Christ to others or to shut him out.

Years ago I read an article by Fr. Eugene Walsh in which he put it simply: "Christ comes to us through us."[1] I've often said that I'd like to see a bumper sticker with that line on it. It would be a good reminder to us that Christ has chosen to be dependent on us for the continuation of his mission. It could keep us alert to the ways that Christ might come to us through other people that we meet on our way through life, and it could also remind us that we are each to be a channel through which Christ can come to others.

Dismissed to the World

At the end of almost every liturgy, the assembly of the baptized is sent forth in a brief rite called the dismissal. It is this rite that gave the Eucharist the common name of the Mass. The term comes from the Latin *missa*, which is part of the dismissal rite. In Latin, the command to the assembly is *Ite, missa est*. In English, our official translation is: "The Mass is ended,

---

[1] Eugene Walsh, "Things Ain't What They Used To Be," *Today's Liturgy* (September–December, 1990) 9.

go in peace." A more literal translation would be: "Go, it is the sending." *Missa* is the root of the word mission. When the liturgy concludes, we are sent forth to carry on the mission.

Some churches have tried to remind themselves of this by posting over the church doors, where it can be seen by those leaving, a sign that reads, "You are now entering mission territory." The mission to which we are all called is not necessarily a mission to foreign lands. Though such international outreach is a mark of a universal Church, there is plenty of mission work to be done in our own society.

Throughout the period of the catechumenate and the period of purification and enlightenment, the catechumens are dismissed from the assembly of the faithful to move to their own assembly to continue breaking open the word. Once they have been initiated into the order of the faithful, however, they are not dismissed until after the eucharistic meal. Having shared at the table of the disciples, they are dismissed now, not to their own assembly, but out into the world to carry the Word of God to others.

These two dismissals can stand as symbols of the dual focus of ministry in the Church. Some ministry is carried out within church organizations and is focused on the needs of members of the Church. The baptized carry on the mission of Christ by catechizing both youth and adults in the parish, by serving in a variety of liturgical ministries, by visiting the sick, by helping the bereaved, by organizing parish social activities and by raising the funds necessary to keep the church open and the programs functioning. They also work with other parishioners to extend Christ's love beyond the parish by serving in soup kitchens, by working in the St. Vincent de Paul Society, by promoting respect for life and by visiting prisoners.

Beyond these various activities, all carried out within or in the name of the parish community, the baptized are called to carry on the work of Christ in the larger world. They need to bring Christian values to bear at work and in school, in neighborhood organizations and political parties, at family gatherings and sporting events. These are the primary arenas where the gospel is lived and where it needs to be preached.

There is a natural tendency to view the ministry of the baptized as primarily what they do in and around the parish. This temptation afflicts the clergy and parish staff members, because these are the activities they can see and they directly involve the staff. It is also a temptation for the laity themselves, because we all suffer from a mental disconnect between church and the rest of life. Fostered in the U.S. by our oft-proclaimed "separation of church and state," this attitude assumes a separation between religion and other areas of life.

The gospel, however, accepts no such separation. Our faith is to influence every part of our lives, and the mission of the baptized is to bring the gospel to bear wherever they live or work or play. Those who live their baptism daily live it during every part of the day wherever life takes them. They are the Body of Christ in the world, and they bring him wherever they go.

For Prayer

Lord, perfect your church in faith and love together with N. our pope, N. our bishop, with all bishops, priests, and deacons, and all those your Son has gained for you. Open our eyes to the needs of all; inspire us with words and deeds to comfort those who labor and are burdened; keep our service of others faithful to the example and command of Christ. Let your Church be a living witness to truth and freedom, to justice and peace, that all people may be lifted up by the hope of a world made new (Eucharistic Prayer for Various Needs and Occasions, IV).

For Reflection and Discussion

1. What image of the Church is dominant for you? Do you think of the order of the faithful as the central order in the Church? Why or why not?

2. Was the idea that all the baptized are responsible for the mission of the Church a new one for you? How do you see yourself carrying on the work of Christ in your life?

3. How would you describe the proper relationship between laity and clergy in the Church?

4. What do you think God is calling you to do at this point in your life? How does God want you to live out your baptismal commitment in the days and years ahead?

5. When you are dismissed from the Mass, do you see yourself as a disciple sent out on a mission? If not, why do you think that is?

6. What do you think is the most helpful idea you gained from this book? What will you do to put it into practice?

Appendix
Suggestions for Parish Leaders

Chapter 1: Fresh from the Font

This series of reflections is addressed directly to parishioners rather than primarily to parish leaders. They are reflective in nature rather than programmatic.

Nevertheless, I hope that they will be useful to parish leadership in a variety of ways. Parish leaders are parishioners, of course, so reflection on our baptismal identity will be beneficial for leaders, too. Parish staffs might even want to spend some time discussing each chapter, looking for personal applications as well as for ideas for enriching parish life.

Those who work with catechumens and candidates for full communion will profit from reflection and discussion of the stages of Christian initiation. Understanding more deeply the purpose and implications of the process and rituals offered in the RCIA will enable catechumenate leaders to guide the initiates into deeper understanding and commitment.

In a similar way, those who prepare parents for the baptism of their children will also find insights here that will be useful. The more that parents understand baptism from the perspective of the catechumenate, the better they will understand their responsibilities in raising their children in the faith. The practice of infant baptism inverts the process, placing the celebration before the process of formation. Seeing that this formation and conversion happen as their children develop is primarily the responsibility of the parents. Helping them deepen their own understanding of the meaning of this sacrament is essential if they are to carry out that task.

Those involved in catechesis in other areas, whether with children or adults, will find in this work much material that can be the basis of formation for their charges. If all of catechesis is ultimately a question of mystagogy, then the content of these reflections might find their place in formation at every level of Christian development.

Chapter 2: The Journey of a Lifetime

The idea that we are a pilgrim people has often been voiced since Vatican II, but it is not clear that people have fully embraced the idea of the Church as a people called to a life of constant growth and change. Many parishes seem to have a stronger attachment to the status quo than to the process of moving toward the kingdom.

Psychologists suggest that excessive attachment to the past often flows from fear of the future. Parish leaders might consider what image of the future they are projecting in the community. Is the future bright with hope or gloomy with threats? What words do you use when speaking of the future? In preaching and catechesis, in parish meetings and planning sessions, is there a strong sense of hope and trust that God is in charge of our future?

In evaluating parish life, consider how closely parish activities are tied to the school year. Do people get the impression that everything begins in September and ends in early June? With the catechumenate in particular, is it clear that the journey continues all year long? In working with catechumens and candidates, is it clear that they are entering on a lifelong journey or are they given the impression that they are entering a short-term program that will end at Easter or Pentecost?

In preparation sessions with parents seeking the baptism of their children, are they given a clear sense that they are committing themselves and their children to an ongoing journey of faith? Do confirmation candidates clearly understand that they are accepting a role within the Church? Do they understand that Christian service is a way of life rather than a requirement to fulfill in order to "graduate" from the confirmation class?

How much attention is given in your parish to the presence and action of the Holy Spirit? Not all Christians need to be charismatic, but all need to be Spirit led. Do you teach both adults and children how to listen to the Holy Spirit? Do parish gatherings, especially where decisions are to be made, begin with prayer for the guidance of the Spirit?

Chapter 3: Becoming a Christian

The concept of conversion may seem like a relatively new idea to many people in the parish, yet many of the elements of conversion have long been part of parish life. We have urged people to avoid sin and to make use of the sacrament of penance to seek forgiveness and overcome habits of sin. We have encouraged prayer and works of charity and use of the sacraments as the means of holiness. We have challenged people to embrace gospel values rather than the values of the world.

What is to be gained, then, by changing our language and grouping these ideas under the rubric of conversion? One value is the grouping itself. Many people do not see a coherent plan of living in the Church's teaching. Often the various elements of our tradition seem to be unconnected or even contradictory. Helping people to see the whole of Christian life as an ongoing process of conversion gives them an organizing concept to grasp the fullness of the gospel message.

Moreover, the regular public celebration of the initial conversion of catechumens provides a natural and powerful reminder to the whole parish of the need for the baptized also to continue their growth in Christ. This enables preachers and catechists working with all groups in the Church to speak a unified message to the whole parish, calling catechumens and candidates and all baptized youth and adults to respond to the word of the Lord and embrace the call to conversion.

Helping people to see conversion as a fundamental lifestyle for all Christians should foster a more open attitude toward change in parish life. The value of such an atmosphere for parish leaders should be obvious. How much time and energy have you expended in the past simply dealing with the assumption that change is a bad thing or a rejection of tradition?

Parish leaders might spend some time evaluating the current attitude of the parish. Is conversion recognized and accepted as a shared challenge for all parishioners, or is it seen as simply a task for catechumens or for candidates "converting" from another denomination? Do staff members of the parish school and the religious education program recognize conversion as the ultimate goal of all their efforts? Do the participants in such programs show evidence of a true conversion of life and values?

A prime time for focusing on conversion, of course, is the season of Lent. As we will see later in chapter 7, the celebration of the scrutinies offers a powerful opportunity to call the whole parish to embrace Christ's call to die to sin in order to experience more fully the new life of the Resurrection. Focusing all Lenten activities in the parish around the concept of personal and parish conversion can help people to enter more deeply into this critical season of the liturgical year.

Chapter 4: Called into Community

Since the Second Vatican Council, parish leaders have used the word community so often that many people have tuned it out. This is partly a result of the power of our cultural tendency toward individualism, which had infected church thinking and practice far more than we may have realized. But it is also partly a result of the fact that we did not find adequate ways to help people understand that Christian faith is communal at its core. Too many people still think of this community emphasis as an "add-on," a nice idea for those inclined to such things, but not essential to being Catholic.

It is ironic that many perceived this emphasis on community as "Protestant" rather than authentically Catholic. The Catholic tradition is much stronger on the communal nature of faith and Christian identity. The Protestant tradition has given more weight to individual interpretation of Scripture and individual conversion experiences than the Catholic tradition. Perhaps it would be helpful to many people to clarify the true shape of the traditional Catholic approach to faith.

On a practical level, people only really understand the communal nature of faith if they have experiences of it. Thus many parishes have found new life through the development of small faith communities. As the number of priests continues to decline and Catholics find themselves grouped in ever-larger parishes, such small faith-sharing groups may be an essential lifeline for sustaining faith and church membership. If your parish has few or no such groups, consider whether it's time to move in that direction.

Images and symbols are powerful tools that shape the identity of the parish and of each member of the faith community. It was in 1943 that Pope Pius XII issued his encyclical *Mystici Corporis*, officially embracing a recovery of that ancient image of the Church. Though the Second Vatican Council highlighted the image of the People of God on pilgrimage (see chapter 2), the image of the Church as the Body of Christ is also present in the council documents. Both images are important. The idea of the People of God supports the involvement of all and the dignity of each member. It also links easily to the notion of our pilgrim status. The image of the Body of Christ stresses the unity of this people and the intimate links between all the members. It also helps avoid a view of the Church as simply a social grouping of individuals by offering a more organic image.

Try keeping track, over a month or so, of how often each of these images finds its way into your speech or writing—in homilies and other worship texts, in the bulletin, in parish meetings, and even in casual conversation. Then ask yourself if the people of your parish really see themselves as one body. How can such awareness be fostered in your situation?

The catechumenate, of course, is a primary locus for fostering such communal awareness. How central has the catechumenate become in your parish life? Is it clear that initiation is the "responsibility of all the baptized"? What can you do to foster fuller interaction between catechumens and candidates and the rest of the community? Those who share in the conversion experience of the initiates come to a new and richer sense of their own faith and recognize the value of sharing faith in community.

Chapter 5: Welcoming the Stranger

Fostering a true spirit of openness in the parish community is usually a difficult task. Besides the natural tendency of people to stay where they are comfortable, many people have come to see religion as one part of their life that should be exempt from the natural laws of change. This is ultimately a foolish expectation, but one that has been encouraged by the Church's official resistance to change in so many areas. Especially before the Second Vatican Council, many church leaders and pastors presented the Church as an unchanging rock. It will take years (probably generations) of consistent catechesis to undo that false image. It is Christ who is our rock, "the same yesterday, today and forever." Everything else is subject to change. As the council noted, the Church is *semper refor-manda*, always to be reformed. Unless we are willing to change in response to God's call, we will soon find ourselves resisting the Lord. This truth needs to be taught consistently to all members of the Church, including those who are in positions of church leadership!

One of the obvious changes facing many parishes is to become more clearly multi-cultural. What different ethnic groups are present in your parish? If you are not sure, how could you determine whether there are small groups of various ethnic backgrounds that are not being adequately recognized and served by the parish and its staff? Even parishes that worship and function in two or three languages may find that there are other groups, not present in large numbers but still having special needs and gifts, that are being overlooked.

Maybe the "others" we need to include are not different in ethnic background but different in economic status. Parishes that are generally middle class may seem unwelcoming to those with fewer financial resources, for example. Poorer parishes may not be very welcoming to wealthy Christians. How could your parish reach out more effectively to such groups? What other forms of discrimination (blatant or subtle) do you detect among members of the parish? How could you invite them to a greater openness?

In urging such broadening, take care to link this movement with personal spiritual growth. Sometimes enunciating moral imperatives simply surfaces guilt and heightens defensiveness. It may be more effective to help people understand the challenge of widening their circle as an invitation by God to deeper spiritual growth, to become more closely identified with their Lord.

A good place to examine the state of things in the parish might be in the catechumenate. Those coming to join the Church bring a variety of impressions and can give you an outsider's perspective on the image the parish presents to the larger community. You might also ask them to evaluate how welcoming the parish seemed when they first approached the community.

After considering how catechumens and candidates are welcomed, you might also discuss how other new members are welcomed to the parish. Do those who are already Catholic get as much attention as inquirers? People moving into the parish have some of the same needs to get to know other parishioners, to understand how the parish functions, to find a place to share their gifts, etc. What might improve that process for newcomers?

Catechumens and candidates are taught the importance of the Scriptures. What opportunities are available for the rest of the parish to deepen their knowledge and appreciation of the Bible? How effectively do preaching and catechesis link the Scriptures and people's daily concerns and decisions?

Chapter 6: Echoing the Word

If the Word of God is to be central in the lives of Christians, parish leaders might ask how central it is in the life of the parish. What opportunities are provided for biblical education and group Bible study in your parish? Is catechesis in the parish at every level based on the word that is proclaimed each Sunday? If not, how can you move in this direction?

We use the sign of the cross so often that it can become an empty gesture. How might the sign of the cross be lifted up in people's awareness? How carefully and deliberately do parish leaders use this ritual gesture, especially during worship? How long has it been since you preached or catechized about its significance?

If the four pillars of catechumenal formation are essential aspects of Christian life, parish leaders should frequently take stock to see how each is being supported in parish programming and structures. Parishes can get out of balance as easily as individual Christians can. How much attention is being paid to each of the four pillars?

A healthy parish has multiple forms of catechesis. What kinds of formation are available in your community? Is as much time devoted to adult formation as to children's catechesis? Do you periodically survey the parish to determine what topics may be of value to the people? Do you provide child care so that couples can participate in formation together? Are there opportunities for multi-generational formation, involving everyone from toddlers to grandparents?

A healthy parish works constantly to foster a sense of community among parishioners. Sometimes this is understood as mere socializing and consists of dances, picnics, bowling, and other parish recreational activities. There is certainly value to such activities, for they encourage parishioners to get to know one another. Beyond recreation, however, consider other ways to foster interaction. Especially in large parishes, many parishioners may not know one another. Whenever parishioners gather for any event, is time devoted to getting acquainted? Are name tags used as often as they might be helpful? Are new parishioners introduced at Mass and linked to "parish sponsors" who can help them get acquainted? Are there opportunities for parishioners to interact in small groups where deeper sharing might occur?

A healthy parish has a variety of opportunities for people to deepen their spiritual growth. A solid liturgical life is fundamental to this, of course. If your parish liturgy is not all that it could be, what is the next step you can take to improve it? Beyond the Eucharist, are there other opportunities for parish prayer? Have morning prayer and/or evening prayer become a regular part of parish life? Does the parish foster a healthy devotional life, in tune with the liturgy? For example, are there special Marian devotions celebrated in connection with the major Marian feasts in the liturgical year? Are there opportunities for spiritual direction available for those who desire such help in their spiritual growth?

A healthy parish has multiple ways for people to serve, both in the parish and in the wider community. As you consider the various ministries within the parish, ask if all of them are open to anyone with the gifts to serve in that capacity or if some are limited to one gender (male ushers, for example) or a certain age group (only adults), etc. How can you make them more inclusive? How many different outreach ministries does the parish have? How are people invited to share in these efforts? Are there other areas of need that are not being met? How can you invite new people to meet such needs? Beyond parish-organized efforts, Christian ministry includes whatever people do at work, at home, and in their neighborhoods to show the love of Christ and proclaim good news. How could the parish better support the efforts of all parishioners in this missionary work?

Chapter 7: Called and Chosen

If parishioners are going to be able to deal in a healthy way with sin and forgiveness, they need a balance between the two main truths discussed in this chapter. Many Christians have an overly negative view of themselves, often because of an overemphasis on sin in past church teaching. Others have reacted against that past approach and gone to the other extreme of denying (at least in practice) the existence of sin in their lives.

It is not easy to maintain the proper balance, but parish leaders can help by regular reference to both. Are your people clearly aware of how much God loves them? Do they see themselves as chosen people, blessed by God beyond measure? If not, perhaps preaching and teaching needs to focus more often on how much God has blessed us. Are your people sufficiently aware of the need for ongoing conversion? Do they use the sacrament of penance in a healthy way? Are they forgiving of others? If not, perhaps teaching and preaching needs to proclaim God's call to repentance and the offer of forgiveness more frequently.

A powerful means of emphasizing both truths in the parish is the full implementation of the Rite of Christian Initiation of Adults. Is the catechumenate really central in the life of the parish? Do people know and interact with the catechumens and candidates throughout the year? If they do, they will likely recognize the catechumen's joy at being called and chosen and will also be drawn to share in their conversion journey.

The conversion dynamic is most fully ritualized in the scrutinies. Are they celebrated in a way that is designed to draw the assembly into the process? Are they celebrated at various Masses so that the whole parish is involved? Are the petitions for the scrutinies based on the real struggles of the catechumens and candidates? Is the whole parish invited to suggest the ways that evil affects our lives? Do those concerns find a place in the petitions, too?

The sacrament of penance is still in need of renewal in most parishes. Are sufficient times available for the individual form of reconciliation? Do parish penance services happen more than once in Advent and once in Lent? Are such services during Lent linked to the scrutinies and/or to the penitential rite for candidates on the Second Sunday of Lent?

Parish leaders who hope to instill both truths in parishioners must have a firm grasp on both in their own lives. Do your pockets carry both messages? How conscious are you on a daily basis that you are called and chosen by God? How seriously do you work on your own conversion?

Chapter 8: Reborn to New Life

As always, the most effective catechesis about sacraments is a full and rich celebration of the liturgy. Parish leaders might spend some time evaluating the celebration of baptism in the parish in all its forms.

Is the Easter Vigil truly the premier liturgical celebration of the year? Does it begin in darkness, with a bonfire drawing people to gather for the opening rites and the procession behind the paschal candle? Does the Liturgy of the Word include a full recounting of salvation history? Does the preaching help people make the connection between this history and their own lives? Is the liturgy of baptism celebrated as fully and richly as possible? Is immersion the norm? Is the symbolism of dying and rising clear and powerful?

Of course, all this will have limited effect if few parishioners come to the vigil. How can you encourage more to gather for this great liturgy? One of the most effective drawing cards is the sense of relationship people have developed with those who will be baptized and received into the Church. How can you foster more interaction between these people and other parishioners?

How and when is infant baptism celebrated? Are infants regularly baptized during Sunday Mass so that the community has frequent access to the power of baptismal symbolism? If baptism is celebrated outside of Mass, are efforts made to gather members of the parish to celebrate with the families? Is baptism always celebrated with music and with a full complement of ministers for the various roles in the liturgy?

If death and resurrection is to be the leitmotif of Christian life, that should be evident in the language used in the parish, especially by parish leaders. You might choose a week and try to be attentive all week to the various ways in which that theme surfaces. Evaluate preaching, prayer texts, catechesis at all levels, the parish bulletin and newsletter, prayer services and devotions, etc. Is the dying and rising of Christ central in the life of the parish?

For people to live their baptismal identity, they need to understand the challenge of living Christianity in contemporary society. What kind of formation is offered to parishioners to help them recognize the difference between the values of society and the values of the Gospel? Is working for social justice and systemic change of our societal structures a regular part of parish life? Do people see such efforts as part of the Church's mission to evangelize the world?

How would you evaluate the balance in parishioners' perspective and in parish activities between the call to embrace death and the invitation to fuller life? Is one more dominant than the other? If so, what needs to be done to achieve better balance between the two?

Chapter 9: Living in the Spirit

The widespread confusion about the proper age for confirmation may have led some parish leaders to shy away from talking much about this sacrament and thus also away from talking much about the Holy Spirit. Though it is difficult to make sense of the varied ages at which we currently celebrate confirmation, this should not prevent a parish from deepening parishioners' awareness of the Spirit's role in a full Christian life. At whatever age confirmation is celebrated, the sacrament is intended to focus our attention on the gift of the Spirit and the role of the Holy Spirit in our lives.

When the parish celebrates confirmation, consider ways to involve the whole parish in the preparation and the celebration. This can be an ideal time to raise awareness of the presence and role of the Holy Spirit among all members of the parish.

Preachers and liturgy planners and catechists should also take full advantage of the Easter season to foster reflection on the meaning of the sacraments of initiation. The readings for the latter Sundays of the season focus increasingly on the Holy Spirit, leading up to the celebration of Pentecost Sunday. Catechesis based on the liturgical year will take full advantage of this liturgical emphasis in the classroom.

Parish leaders might examine catechetical programs in the parish to see if they give adequate attention to the Holy Spirit.

This should go beyond looking at printed materials to consider catechists' own awareness, prayer used in catechetical sessions, etc. Special attention should be given, of course, to confirmation preparation programs to see if they treat confirmation properly, making clear its connection to baptism.

Parish leaders might spend some time sharing with each other their own awareness of the Holy Spirit and their experience (or lack thereof) of listening for the voice of the Spirit. Parish staff meetings might regularly begin with some time of silent listening, followed by prayer for the guidance of the Spirit in decisions made during the meeting. It might be a good idea to develop a similar practice for all parish groups— pastoral and finance councils, parish commissions, ministry groups, etc.

It might also be helpful to teach people the traditional prayer to the Holy Spirit (see *Catholic Household Blessings and Prayers*, 157). Such a prayer might be used in dialog form at parish meetings, but it is also useful for individual prayer, especially if it is memorized by parishioners. Encouraging people to begin their day with this prayer could significantly increase their awareness of the Spirit's presence throughout the day.

Some parishes have developed procedures for choosing pastoral council members based on discernment rather than elections. Such a process can sensitize the entire parish to the role of the Spirit in discernment. Careful discernment of the progress of catechumens through the stages of the catechumenate is another opportunity to raise awareness of our dependence on the Holy Spirit.

If we want parishioners to live a deeply spiritual life, parishes need to offer opportunities for spiritual direction, retreats, days of recollection, etc. Sometimes we can get so focused on maintaining parish structures and organizations that we can forget that growth in holiness should be a major purpose of parish life. More attention to this area can heighten awareness of the role of the Spirit. Such opportunities should include teaching people how to listen for and recognize the voice of the Holy Spirit.

Chapter 10: Gathered Around the Table

There has been much concern in recent years about reports that some Catholics do not believe that the bread and wine truly become the body and blood of Christ. There is a need in every age, of course, for adequate catechesis on this fundamental truth of our faith.

Yet if that is the full extent of our catechetical efforts, the people of God will be deprived of much of their birthright in regard to this central sacrament of the Church. People also need to be offered the richness of the tradition about the meaning and purpose of this sacrament. The link between the sacramental body of Christ and the mystical body should be clearly taught and often recalled. Parishioners also need to understand the sacrificial nature of the Mass and the way that the liturgy itself urges us to give of ourselves, both in worship and in daily life.

Parish leaders should regularly evaluate the catechetical efforts in the community to ensure that they adequately convey the full tradition about the Eucharist. This should encompass everything from First Communion classes to the adult catechumenate.

The celebration of First Communion in the parish is a prime opportunity to catechize children, their parents, and the whole community. This presumes, of course, that the celebration makes clear that First Eucharist is a sacrament of initiation into the Church's ongoing liturgical life. Too often the event is perceived as being a miniature version of a wedding rather than the beginning of an ongoing pattern of eucharistic sharing. Parishes should make clear the link to baptism (and confirmation) and emphasize that these children are taking another step into full membership in the Body of Christ.

If the parish is to be eucharistic to its core, then it needs a strong awareness of God's generous love. It is good news that we are called to preach, and that good news is centered on God's overwhelming love that forgives our sinfulness and gives us the fullness of life.

Some people claim that the emphasis on God's love after the Second Vatican Council reduced the Church's teaching to emotional superficiality. If there is any truth in the claim, the proper response is not to stop preaching this good news but to preach and teach it more fully and more deeply. There is no other adequate basis for faith and for parish life. If what we do is not motivated by gratitude to God, then it can hardly claim to be a response to the Gospel.

One of the hazards of our culture, of course, is that the abundance of material goods at our disposal can blind us to our dependence on God. It is so easy to forget that all is gift and to begin to think of our possessions as ours by right because we've earned them. Parish leaders who have a strong sense of thanksgiving to God can set a tone in the parish that consistently rejoices in God's gifts and invites all to share their sense of gratitude.

Chapter 11: What Have I Done?

Every year during the Easter season parishes have a prime opportunity to help the baptized deepen their understanding of the significance of the sacraments of initiation in their daily lives. Obviously, the effectiveness of this period of mystagogical reflection will depend on how well and how deliberately it is prepared each year.

It is possible, of course, to celebrate the Sundays of Easter with little attention to the newly baptized and the meaning of the sacraments. Many parish leaders do not yet understand the intent and the potential of this festal season. If that is the case in your parish, you might begin by gathering parish leaders and studying together what the Rite of Christian Initiation of Adults says about the period of mystagogy. Time spent reflecting upon and discussing the readings of the Sundays of Easter can lead to deeper awareness of how these readings (especially in Year A, but in all three cycles) support ongoing reflection on the sacraments and the meaning of Christian initiation.

Preachers hold a central key to using this period well. Preaching throughout Easter should continually link the experiences of the newly baptized with the lives of the rest of the baptized. Allowing the newly baptized to share something of their experience of initiation as part of the homily may also be an effective way to invite others to enter into the realm of mystery.

Those who prepare and preside at sacramental celebrations need a vital awareness of the potential for encounter with mystery within these liturgies. Such awareness will enable them to avoid a style that is too casual and to encourage true prayerfulness among the assembly. Planners and liturgical ministers should pay special attention to the role of silence within the various liturgical rituals. Adequate shared silence can do much to heighten the assembly's awareness of the divine presence and thus foster the possibility of encounter with the mystery.

What is needed, at root, is continual attention to mystery. It is all too easy for a parish to spend much time and effort talking about God and Christ and the Spirit without really providing much opportunity for people to personally encounter the Trinity. Parish leaders might examine themselves and their ministries to see whether they reflect an openness to encounter with the divine. A heightened awareness among the parishioners may need to begin with a heightened awareness among parish leaders.

Chapter 12: Looking Back, Looking Forward

Though most Catholics do not have personal memories of their own baptisms, they have an opportunity every year to renew their baptismal commitment publicly. The renewal of baptismal promises is part of the celebration of Easter, but it can be insignificant if it is treated casually. Presiders and liturgy planners should consider carefully how to highlight the importance of this moment each year. Perhaps more important than any liturgical variations is to focus Lent in a way that leads people toward this moment as a true profession of faith and reaffirmation of baptism.

As we noted earlier, of course, the celebration of baptism in the midst of the parish community is an effective way to allow people to reclaim the meaning of their own baptisms throughout the year. Formation of parents before the baptism of their children should include some reflection on the witness they give by bringing their children into the midst of the parish for this pivotal moment. Parents thus can be urged to minister to the community at the same time the community is ministering to them and their child.

Parish leaders might also spend some time reflecting together on the dignity of the order of the faithful and their role in the mission of the Church. Often the language we use in daily parish life reveals unexamined assumptions about the relationship between clergy and laity or professional staff and volunteers. Examining these assumptions can be spiritually healthy as well as challenging. Consider how your parish life and staff activity might change if the order of the faithful was truly treated as the most important part of the Church.

For members of the faithful to fully embrace their mission, it must be clear that the parish sees itself as having a mission. Too often parish life can become mostly inward-looking, concerned only about parish members and their needs. Parish leaders should regularly step back and evaluate how much of parish activity is directed outward toward those who do not yet belong and those who do not know Christ.

Parishioners also need guidance and support for carrying the Gospel into the workplace and neighborhood. Consider the possibility of small faith communities or "mission support groups" organized by profession or by neighborhood or by family status (singles, couples without children, those with young children, those with teens, etc.). Consider inviting parishioners to witness to their efforts to bring the Gospel to the world, perhaps as part of the homily or in the bulletin or in another forum.